Conquering

Dyslexia

Theo Gough

Published by New Generation Publishing in 2019

First Edition

ISBN 978-1-78955-585-1

www.newgeneration-publishing.com

New Generation Publishing

CONTENTS

ACKNOWLEDGMENTS

In this part I want to acknowledge everyone who got me to this place, and most of all I want to acknowledge my mum and dad for working with me and fighting the battles that I couldn't fight.

Thank you to Browns School and all the caring teachers there for helping me with my dyslexia.

Thank you Tony Robbins for helping me and millions of others; I will be forever in your debt, and I want to say a massive thank you to everyone who helped me create and edit this book, Thank you to people John Williams who helped me see the opportunities of publishing my book.

Thank you to my dad, David Gough and Rebecca Elkan for helping with editing the start of the book and to Sinhéidin Goguel for spending hundreds of hours spell checking and editing the book.

Part 1:

My story!

Chapter 1

Every dyslexic person has their own story.
This is my story; my story of discovery.
My story of taking ownership and realising that my so-called disability is my greatest gift.

On 22nd July 2018, 6 weeks after I was born, all my limbs started to shake sporadically. My parents took me to Kings College Hospital for children immediately. They were so scared and didn't have a clue what was happening to the newest addition of their family.

The Doctor, Mr King, said to my parents –

Your child has clones!

He explained to them that this is where some of the nerve endings had not fully developed yet. And reassured them that I would soon grow out of it and they would develop.

Mum...
Theo was an enormous baby, 90th percentile size and health. He grew rapidly. Breast feeding was short lived, much to my disappointment, and a lifelong relationship with food began..

As early as 18 months it was noticed I had a speech delay. I couldn't form any recognisable sounds yet, and never came close to sounding out words. Everyday both my mum and dad longed for me to say those words –

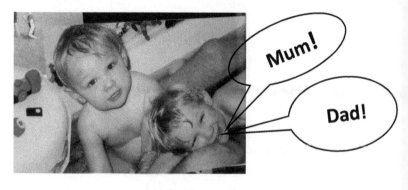

They put it down to slow development and thought I would catch up.

In January 2003, when I was 3, my grandparents could see that my speech was not developing at all. They only saw me twice a year, as they lived far away, and noticed that I hadn't developed my speech but my older brother, Luke and three older cousins had.

Mum...

Theo grew very fast. He was difficult to understand and he was clumsy. Lots of accidents! But he was so lovely, kind and happy, he had a wonderful caring nature. He was easy to love and eager to make friends and have a laugh.

Theo's speech progressed so slowly. His sounds were so mixed up and boy did he speak fast. Initially I believed he was just a slow developer, he would catch up at some point!

I believed speech therapy would help. A bit of extra practise and he would be ok.

They said to my mum and dad -

'Theo's speech is not improving at all. He sounds the same as when he was 18 months. There have been no changes! None whatsoever!'

Next, to take notice was my Nursery, in April 2003. They gave me Speech and Language therapy, in a small group of 4, twice a week.

In the same year my parents broke up. My mum put an offer on a house in Keston, Kent and sold the house in Croydon. My mum, brother and I moved from our five story house in Croydon

to a lovely 3 bedroom house in a little village. There was a school just a minute down the road, opposite some woods.

As you can imagine this was a very scary and uncertain time for my mum. Not knowing what would happen if she didn't get the

house. Luckily she got the house and I got into Year One in the school on our doorstep. It looked like the perfect fit for me as it was a one form entry. All together the school had about 120 pupils. The fewer children meant more attention and support for my speech and language needs.

The school quickly picked up on my very low stage of development in English. My first Individual Education Plan (IEP) started in January 2005 and I successfully failed to meet the targets set in every single IEP from year one to year four. I think they gave up after that!

Chapter 2

Walt Disney died before the opening of Disneyland.
One man said, 'isn't it a shame he can't be here to see it?'
His friend replied 'No! He saw it first and that's why you are seeing it now.'

Walt Disney

Every child is born with a vivid imagination. But just as a muscle grows flabby with disuse, so the bright imagination of a child pales in later years if he ceases to exercise it.

From a young age, I was aware that in school and at home, I had a very short attention span and my imagination let's say was not limited by anything. I remember often feeling like I was in a completely different world and that with a flick of a switch I could change my reality from seeing everyday boring life to being on a battle ground or in a superhero fight and use my powers which were virtually limitless.

When I was playing football, with my friends, I used to zone out into a different world for the whole game and imagine that the football pitch was a battleground and I was fighting dragons. I would shoot massive red hot fireballs from my hands to take down the dragons, meanwhile dodging all the flames of fire from the dragons. I would be able to bend the earth to my will. I would pick up massive chunks of earth and launch it straight at the dragons.

I would not have a clue what was happening in the game of football and as I was often the goalie this was not liked by my team. Perhaps this was the reason I never made the school football team and it wasn't my lack of speed or skills!

I always had a unique ability to use seemingly basic objects, like a glove or a pencil, in some elaborate story that could go on for hours. When I used to play with my friends we'd pretend that we had superpowers but I didn't feel like I was pretending. My friend had the power to be superfast and I had the ability to be super strong and do incredible feats of strength like taking a whole tree out of the ground. I genuinely believed that I had this superpower. I would go home and think about stopping cars with my hands, beating up the toughest man on the planet, and punching a hole through concrete.

> Mum...
> Taking Theo out shopping was worrying! Well actually taking Theo anywhere was a nightmare! After a very scary and worrying incident where I lost him in Glades Shopping Centre and security not being able to understand him, I was advised to give him a name card with his home phone number in his pocket, just in case I lost him again.

Back then I didn't know if I was dreaming or not! For years, I believed there was a working shower in the middle of the woods near my house and we would go down there and take a shower and when we were actually walking in the woods I would go looking for it. I did this for years. I never found the shower!

7

As to my imagination and my ability to go to a completely different world, I'm glad to say I still have this at a very active level. I will let you in on a little secret, that only my closest friends or family know. In my house, I have a basket full of sticks that I found in the

woods and toy weapons that I sometimes still play fighting games with.

I imagine a completely different world with goodies and baddies.

And while I'm here, I might as well tell you another secret. I also have a basket full of toy figures by the toilet for when I get bored.

When people come over to the house they often ask

why is there a basket full of action figures by the toilet and why are there sticks and plastic swords in the kitchen.

I say –

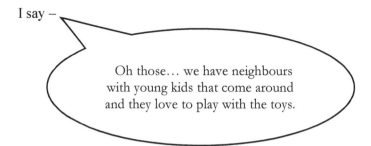

Oh those… we have neighbours with young kids that come around and they love to play with the toys.

Most of my inspiration comes from films and videos I see. Over time the stories have become very complex; with different time periods, different worlds, many characters and many powers. If I wrote them all down they would make a collection of books.

In school I often found things very confusing. Many times I didn't know why the teacher was telling me off. Even now, not much has changed in the way I think and process information. I find social interaction with more than two people hard. I find it hard to keep up with the different threads of the conversation. I feel confident speaking to one person but as soon as there are more people in the room I find it very hard to keep track of the conversation and know what is going on and often come out with random comments that I'm thinking of but have no real relevance to the conversation.

I had a weird obsession with 'mines', my name for a baby's teething blanket. Until now I had no idea what purpose they had but now I know! I often see a child in a push buggy sucking on one and this brings me back to the days I couldn't go anywhere without mine.

Mum...

As he grew, he began to lose his happy disposition. His relationship with the world changed. He couldn't communicate with it. It seemed that his memory was non-existent. He couldn't remember where he lived or his phone number and couldn't pronounce his own name although he was 8.

My first spoken word was when I was reaching out for my white blanket and said *'MINE'*. From that moment these blankets will be known for ever as *'mine'* to me. I loved *'mines'* for years and years. I put my thumb in my mouth while smelling my *'mine'*. It was very comforting. I had my *'mine'* with me even in school plays, in class, when going to sleep. I couldn't leave the house without my *'mine'* and always wrapped it around my hand. Each birthday and Christmas after that I would get a new 'mine', and they were the best gifts ever. Surprisingly, I would never lose my *'mine'* but I would lose everything else.

After a couple of years I had collected enough *'mines'* to make into a big ball held together by knots. This ball came everywhere with me. My precious *'mines'* are now safe in the loft.

Chapter 3

*'Everyone is a genius. But if you judge a
fish on its ability to climb a tree, it will
live its life believing it is stupid.'*
Albert Einstein

School got a lot tougher in Year One. In Reception and Nursery it was all playing about in sandpits with dinosaurs, having stories read to us when all we had to do was repeat back what we heard which was so hard for me. Having playtime to break up short sessions of work then back to play was ideal for me. But now I was a big kid, now we had real lessons, real work.

'Mum...

He was always the tallest in any play group, in nursery and in primary school.

This meant unfortunately as his needs grew more apparent, and his confidence disappeared he couldn't hide. Everyone thought he was older than he was, and they added, he should be more able.

The opposite couldn't have been more true!

As the class moved on and progressed onto breaking down words into sounds and using sounds to make up words, I didn't!

I couldn't say the sound not to mind put lots of them together to make a word!

I noticed that other kids in my class were making lots of progress but not me! All the other kids got stickers to put on their sticker chart, but not me! I would hear the teachers saying well done to all the kids and showing the whole class how well they had done, but this was never me!
I would dream of the teacher showing my work to the whole class and seeing how smart I was, but dreaming was all that ever happened!
All the teachers ever said to me was: focus more, try a little harder, try this, do it this way and you can do it Theo, I believe in you.

I remember thinking the kids in Keston are so smart. I didn't think I was dumb. I just thought all the kids were so smart. With each passing day, as all the other kids got better and better, the expectations of the teachers got lower and lower of me. My table was separated from the others so I could focus more! The teachers stopped correcting my work regularly, stopped saying try this and worst of all stopped saying: I believe in you!

After a few months I thought,

They can't all be so smart.

I started shutting myself off from the rest of the world. I became more and more shy. I was so nervous and scared that the teacher would ask me to read or write something on the board. Every time my teacher used to come close to my desk, my hands used to shake and my palms used to sweat uncontrollably. It became harder and harder to breath. As my throat closed up, I would feel the worst butterflies in my stomach that would make me want to throw up. This happened like clockwork every time the teacher used to come close to my desk. I was so terrified that they would see my blank piece of paper during the lesson and tell everyone else and the whole class would see how dumb I was.

Mum...

At school the teachers were increasingly confused. They couldn't grasp all the complexities. There were so many issues. His speech was jumbled, but also he had no memory. However many times he repeated something like a sound, it was all forgotten within a couple of minutes. He was good with numbers, he was even very able. This confused people more. The educational psychologist, (Ms Thomson), saw him several times but all her recommendations didn't seem to improve matters.

I remember years of Letterland and alphabet posters. Years of a relentless regime of praise through repetition and completing sheets. But CH, SH, W, R, TH and F etc

The same feelings came when we were reading aloud in class; standing up and taking turns. When we weren't reading aloud we were to follow the story and read silently. After my sweating and shaking with fear died down I would pick up the book with the most pictures in that I could find and pretend that I was reading it. I would mimic how the others were reading by moving my eyes from left to right of the page to make it look like I was reading. I used to see other people and cartoons on the TV moving their eyes from left to right when they were reading so that is what I did.

Other children and adults always used to ask me where I

was from. I would get confused and think to myself why are they asking me this question.

They had trouble believing me.

This was because I had trouble in learning to speak and my sounding out of words was so poor they thought I must not be English. I didn't even notice it myself at the time.

Before long I had feelings of dread. A deep feeling I was different, feeling useless and self-conscious of what other people thought of me. As a result my body posture changed dramatically. My head was down looking to the floor; my shoulders were slumped and caved in. I was a hunchback waiting to happen. My

Mum....

Theo's real problem growing up at this time was not his dyslexia. We didn't even know he had dyslexia. Theo could understand us but it took him years to realise that we couldn't understand him. Theo couldn't pronounce certain sounds. The 'sh', 'ch' was mixed 'w' and 'r' was muddled and didn't have a hope with 'th', 'w' 'f'.

Speech therapy was started in nursery, and a relentless regime of practise through repetition and colouring sheets began at home.

grandad used to say to me, if you keep looking down like that your head will get stuck there for good.

My temper got increasingly worse; I started losing it at home over the littlest of things. I would yell at my mum and get into fights with my brother.

I remember one Sunday, when on a family day out, I chased my bother around an arcade with a big old metal spade.

These outbursts of anger were frustration and a way for me to express the feelings inside me. Before long my anger moved to school. It got to a point where I couldn't hold my feelings back and out of

Mum...

I don't think I've ever felt as unprepared and lacking in knowledge as I did then; trying to understand which direction to go in and the steps to take.

nowhere I would just get into strops and not do anything in lessons, not play with anybody and reject anybody who tried to help me or make me feel better.

I became more and more cut off from the rest of the world. I just wanted to be invisible. I didn't play at play time. I was being told off more and more often and got into trouble and did not understand why or what for. I was a mess.

I hated myself and everything around me.

I pushed away all my friends and had quickly gained the reputation of that kid who was always in a bad mood. I often used to overhear other children saying –

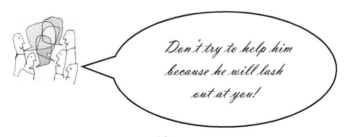

Don't try to help him because he will lash out at you!

This was my way of coping with feeling so stupid, feeling different, feeling worthless. Having people say I was a bully or a bad kid was much less painful than people thinking I was different and bullying me because I was dumb. It was my way of distracting people from seeing what I couldn't do. It was my choice to be a bully and a bad kid.

I chose to hurt them first before they had the chance to hurt me!

At this point my stomach was hurting most of the day and I never had an appetite. I would lay in my bed for hours feeling scared and worried about my future. I would worry about whether I even had a future. I would ask myself –

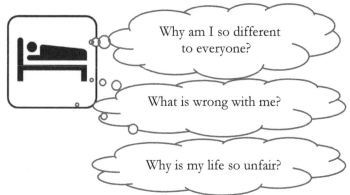

Why am I so different to everyone?

What is wrong with me?

Why is my life so unfair?

I drove myself crazy with these questions and was losing sleep every night.

One sunny Monday afternoon, in July 2004, after another dreadful day passed at school, I was walking home with my mum. We only lived minutes away from my school so it was an easy, short walk home. She held my hand and was trying to make small talk with me to cheer me up. With my head down and my chin touching my chest, my shoulders slumped and back arched, I was not listening to her at all. Not responding.

Despite this my mum was persistent and didn't give up. She was telling me stories about our new puppy, a golden retriever called Hannah.

HANNAH, NOW 13!

She told me that Hannah was eating all the ice-creams from all the other families in the park and was getting fat.

As we turned the corner to walk up the steps to our house I grabbed her hand tightly and looked up into her eyes. Struggling to breath and with a red, tear stained face I croakily whispered,

Mum...I wish I was dead....
I wish that I was never born!

This was the tipping point for my parents. They were more motivated than ever to find out what was wrong with me and get the proper support and help I so desperately needed.

Chapter 4

The biggest problem with dyslexics is not dyslexia itself but our perception of what dyslexia means to us. That was my biggest problem.

In year 3 I had a wonderful teacher called Ms Ross. She was also the school's special needs coordinator (SENCO). We agreed to properly start the formal process of getting me a statement, which would provide the school with extra money to support my learning journey.

I remember mum being incredibly sad and in a low mood for weeks. She, herself remembers a horrible feeling of depression setting in. She knew I wasn't catching up, and nobody could clearly tell her what was wrong. Nobody!

Mum...

I remember a total feeling of dread. The school process was so slow. Working in a school myself, I knew this. Theo was also my child, and he was ultimately my responsibility and it was down to me to do everything in my power to help him.

Mum...

I quickly realised I could not do this alone! I quickly forgave his dad for the unpleasant divorce so we could work together. It had never been my intention to take Theo out of mainstream education. I was happy to work with Keston School and they themselves did everything they could but things were just getting worse. I could see Theo disappearing into himself, getting so sad and hurting so much. He needed me. I felt like holding his hand and never letting go.

My mum had enough and started taking matters into her own hands. The school were doing everything they could.

From practically the first day I started at Keston School I got sent to psychologist after psychologist, speech and language specialist after speech and language specialist and had IEP plans filling my ears.

Mum told me recently all of the assessments, the first term at Brown's and the court case to fight for my statement cost her and dad £18,000. However, I was still depressed, still couldn't sleep, and had trouble speaking and no hope in the classroom.

One day my mum had an epiphany! She remembered she kept the letter from the paediatric doctor from my birth, saying I had colon disease and used this to get my next referral.

Soon afterwards we got a letter in the post with the next step. The letter the doctors sent to my parents requested that I stay awake the night before so I would fall asleep for the scan, It was an ECG scan. Before I fell asleep the nurses stuck little magnetic discs, called electrodes, on my head and turned on the monitoring screen. I don't remember much else as I fell asleep. They told me afterwards, they had monitored me while I was sleeping and nothing alarming showed up but we would need to get the full report from the consultant.

We waited tentatively for 3 weeks, to get the results. We received a letter inviting my parents and myself to meet the consultant to discuss the results of the ECG. My mum, dad and I all gathered into a large consulting room where the neurological doctor opened a file, took out an envelope, opened it and then looked at my parents and said,

> Yes… there is damage to his left hemisphere with OOPS… oh wrong envelope! This is yours… NO is fine here.

This really happened!

Next, he added that they would look over the results and come to a decision.

They carried on referring me. The next step and final option was to refer me to a chartered psychologist to find out why I couldn't read, write or speak properly. This was where everything changed. Valerie Muter changed my life forever.

When I was 8 years old, on the 16th October 2007, my mum, dad and I travelled to Valerie Muter's house in East London. I loved her house. She had a whole room with just toys in it. The room was full of Lego, race cars, bricks. It just had everything you could imagine, a kids dream.

As luck would have it, just after I started to get out the Lego it was time to do the tests. 3 hours later we stopped to have lunch. After which another 2 long hours of assessments, with only 5 minutes break in the middle took place.

At the end of a very long day of tests, I was absolutely zonked. Valerie said I could go play in the games rooms for as long as I wanted. I couldn't believe my ears and all of a sudden I was excited and full of energy again.

Next, Valerie pulled together 3 multi-coloured kids chairs - one for mum, one for dad and the middle one for me. She sat near us all, in a bigger adult's chair. I didn't sit in it for long as I was too busy playing with Lego and toy cars.

Valerie said to my parents–

The reason no one has been able to put their finger on the reason why Theo is not developing his speech and literacy skills is because he has a combination of different complex specific learning difficulties.

She went on to say –

Theo has very severe developmental dyslexia disorder combined with a speech and language disorder, visuomotor difficulties, which is just a complex way of saying the brain processes movement differently which affects his handwriting, and finally immature attention skills. Let me show you....

She pulled out a piece of paper and started by drawing 4 circles overlapping in the middle. Then she pointed to the middle and said this represents Theo.

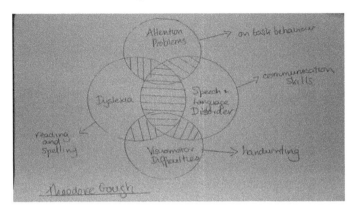

She then added that because of my complex needs I would need special full-time education to help cope. She looked at my parents with a sensitive smiled and they nodded.

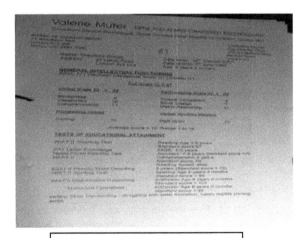

Caption of the long, but fundamental report that changed everything!

Here is a small part of the report to give you a flavour:

....*Theo is a little boy of normal intelligence with a severe and complex learning difficulty. This comprises of a number of learning difficulties. First Theo is significantly dyslexic, in combination with phonological ie speech sounds processing and phonic decoding difficulties. In addition, Theo has poor fine mother skills which of course are affecting his hand writing. Finally Theo shows immature attention skills...*

Just as we were about to leave Valerie gave me a gift! She got out of her chair and kneeled down so she was eye level with me. She took my hands and with a massive smile, she said,

Theo you have an amazing gift!
You have dyslexia. Do you know some of the most successful people are dyslexic! Albert Einstein was

I smiled with the biggest grin from ear to ear.

I walked away that day being so happy, so happy that I had dyslexia.

My mum and dad were so relieved. They were so relieved because they had some answers. They had results. Yes it wasn't the happiest of news initially. And yes I would need a lot of extra help and support throughout my education, but at least my parents knew where to look.

My parents were no longer blindly stabbing in the dark, no longer taking me to see specialist after specialist trying to find out why their 8 year old son was so depressed and struggling to communicate his feelings and

ley didn't accept me.

The final summary of their report read,

....Ideally Theo should be taught in a one to one setting as often as possible. However, he would benefit most if he was to be placed in a dyslexic friendly school. This would enable him to have every opportunity to reach his potential.....

My mum and dad's facial expressions changed and I could see they were gutted. Imagine how they felt if the top dyslexic institute in London could not help their son how the hell could they.

My mum and dad were devastated with this latest news.

But they didn't give up on me. Somehow they carried on searching for the help I so badly needed. With a stroke of luck my mum made friends with one of the other parents at Keston School. Her name was Sharia.

She told mum about her son who has dyslexia and that he was attending Browns School. My mum asked more about it. Sharia explained that it was a special needs school for children with dyslexia. She said it's amazing - it's got 30 kids, 20 fulltime teachers, a big field for the children to play and a lovely

Mum...

For me the tipping point came at the beginning of year 4. I visited Theo at school. He was all alone on a computer doing nothing. The class teacher told me "Theo was doing fine! FINE! I don't think I'd ever seen such a sad lonely boy, sitting all alone, head so low, that was doing fine! Please may I leave I replied.

This was a crystal clear realisation. Theo was never going to have a chance in life if he was to stay in this environment, and any amount of extra hours of help was not going to change anything.

head teacher called Mr Brown. The best thing is that it's not too far; it's only in Chesterfield, a 15 minute car journey away. She encouraged mum to check it out. My mum said she definitely would.

My mum knew this was my only shot and dad agreed. They knew I would never get an opportunity like this again and if I got in, my life would never be the same. They immediately called up and arranged a meeting with Mr Brown.

At this point, I had been at Keston for over 3 years surrounded by letters, foreign words, confusing instructions and an increasing self-awareness that I was dumb and different. How could any more well-meaning interventions help?

Chapter 5

'I think everything about my life is magical. I've struggled, and against most odds, I'm truly having the experience of living my dream'.

Bella Thonne

At the end of my first meeting with the head of Browns, Mr Brown wasn't confident that the school could give me the support I needed. He said to my parents that out of his 18years experience of running a dyslexic school he had only seen 2 other children with needs as severe as mine. This was surprising, since more than half the number of pupils, were full time trained teachers. Not giving up on me he gave me a week's trial and luckily they accepted me.

However, there was one big problem. It cost **£25,000** a year to attend the school. This was not affordable for my parents.

On the first of January 2008, my mum sent a letter to Keston School saying that my needs were too severe for them and Theo needed full time support in education. A month later mum took me out of Keston with very short notice and put me into Browns School. She didn't have the money to pay for it, but she knew that it was the best thing for me; she knew it was the only chance for me to have a fighting chance at life.

My parents pulled together all the paper work, assessments and diagnoses over the years and went to Bromley Council to get me a statement that proved my needs could not be addressed in a regular state school. This statement would fund the individual support and help I needed to make progress. I needed Bromley

Council to support a statement so I could stay at Browns School without my parents becoming bankrupt. Unfortunately, they took some convincing and my parents fought against the local council and Keston School. Damn did my parents fight hard with endless blood, sweat, tears and money; accumulating costs of over £18,000 for the first term at Browns and fighting the council.

Mum...

The court case was not to get Theo a statement, Keston School were already working on that. He was going to get a statement but the court case was for where the money for the statement was going to go i.e. where Theo was going to go to school. I wanted Theo to go to Browns School but Keston wanted to get a statement and keep him at Keston, so then they would get to keep the money for themselves. They were very upset and angry when I took Theo out of the school because I was taking money out of the school as well. I will never forget Lindsay's words. The 'matter of fact' way she said it. Finally we won. At last I could finally breathe. At last he was safe. He was surrounded by the kindest, warmest, most understanding staff and little, by little over many months, his head rose up and wasn't so low. As part of this ugly battle we had Lindsey Peer, who was part of the solicitor's team. She was a chartered psychologist helping us prove my son's needs. She told me that Theo was in the top 2% of the severest dyslexics; with a sore of 0.5%. She then said this makes Theo one of the most severe dyslexics in England. An awkward silence filled the room as I struggled to hear and comprehend this.

There were big obstacles along the way with the biggest being the court case. This went on for months and even included my old head teacher fighting against us and insisting I went back to a state school. However, my severe needs shone through and we thankfully won the case and I received my statement. This statement meant that my parents wouldn't have to pay for my needs but the council would pay for it, so I could get the right support in my education.

> Mum...
>
> By February 2008 Theo, started his new school, Browns. This was around the time it had been recommended to us to contact a lawyer or a barrister. This of course got worse!
>
> The worse the result the

My very first day at Browns School is etched into my memory forever. My body was full of nerves and I felt so scared. I was thinking here we go again as I walked in through the school gates. My head was down, my back was arched, my chest and shoulders were down and slumped and my anxiety about the future was as high as ever. I believed I was stupid, dumb and retarded, and these thoughts or should I say labels were running full speed around my head. There was no hope for me. I put on an act for my parents because I didn't want them to see how I was really feeling. I knew that it would have made them feel even worse.

I was the shyest person you have ever seen. I had no confidence at all. I didn't speak to anyone. I kept myself all to myself even when people came up to me and try to befriend me. They would say,

'Hi, my name is Sam, what's your name?'

I would look them up and down. Not say anything and walk away with my head hanging low.

But all of that changed just for a moment halfway

through that day. I was sitting alone in the reading corner with all kinds of big colourful picture books around me. I was minding my own business in my little happy place and when I'm in my happy place I forget my surroundings and I stick my finger up my nose!

Out of the corner of my eye I saw this big figure standing there. Her name was Miss Kelly. As I saw her looking at me I quickly pulled my finger out of my nose as fast as I could, hoping she didn't see where my finger actually was. As I cautiously looked up at her, she had this big smile on her face. She said in a calming and loving voice,

'Theo, there are lots of nose pickers here! You will fit right in!'

The biggest grin from ear to ear spread across my face and then myself and Miss Kelly burst out laughing.

'Just in that one moment I felt happy. I felt like I belonged somewhere.'

Chapter 6

'In the middle of difficulty lies opportunity.'
Albert Einstein

I was now eight years old and that was the first time I can remember in the whole of my schooling feeling happy to be there. This was the first brick in building my wall of confidence. But that was not enough to build a whole wall. The rest of that day was much like the first part but I did have one happy memory to bring home with me.

That first day was nerve wrecking and in my head I was thinking here we go again! I was still terrified of the future.

Over months and years Browns School gave me extraordinary help, they gave me everything I needed at that time.

I got placed a year below where I should have been. Instead of taking a place in year 4, I was placed in year 3. The reason was to help me cope with my reading and writing.

I didn't understand why at the time and my teacher said to me:

> WE DON'T HAVE ENOUGH CHAIRS IN YEAR 4 FOR YOU TO FIT IN THE CLASS THEO, BUT WE HAVE AN EXTRA ONE IN YEAR 3.

I fully believed this and I kept on saying this to people for years.

I was always in the very lowest class for English with only two or three others. Sometimes, due to my extremely low level in reading and writing, they even had to make special lessons just for me. This was perfect because it gave me the support and emotional care I needed.

To make matters even worse, by this time I had developed a stutter. So even though I couldn't pronounce my words correctly because I had a speech impediment, I developed a stutter so I couldn't even say the words that were not pronounced right. For this Browns gave me 1 to 1 speech correction classes that I did for years.

Out of every class this was the one that I hated the most. For one hour a week, sometimes more, I would go into a room with a teacher and feel like an idiot. I would practise sounding out sounds like

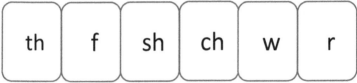

and many more sounds.

Because of the way I felt about the class my learning was painfully slow. It was so slow that in fact it took me 6 long years of one to one lessons before I could say my name 'Theo' correctly!

My strategy of learning was there however my reasons for learning weren't!

FACT!
It took me 6 long years of one to one lessons before I could say my name 'Theo' correctly!

Yes I couldn't even say my name correctly. I used to say 'Feo' with an 'F' sound and not 'Th' sound. I always thought people used to say my name wrong!

I used to say, 'My name isn't Feo it's Feo!'

I practised saying 'Th' an 'F' over and over. Week after week, month after month and year after year until I could say my name fluently and correctly.

Only some months ago, my mum admitted to me that:

FUN FACT!

...for years she didn't have a clue what I was saying. I used to talk to her for 15 minutes straight with such passion and enthusiasm about whatever I was talking about and my mum didn't have the heart to tell me she didn't understand a single word I was saying. She would just smile and nod her head!

Can you imagine if you couldn't say your name correctly for your whole life?

Every year I did the same English test paper and every year it was the same outcome they would share with my parents -

'Theo is making slow but steady progress.'

It was extremely slow and steady!

This was not because of a lack of effort on Browns part.

Some of the things they did to help me improve my

At reading time I played board games with the teacher that were designed to help me with different aspects of my English.

English were:

In my one to one lessons I used to draw letters and words in the air with my finger and imagine the word and say it out loud as I was drawing it.
I made letters and words out of clay and then when the clay was set I used to practise reading the words.
I drew letters and words in the sand and say the word
In class we would say letters of a word out loud and then say the word over and over. For example we would repeat C,A,T CAT C,A,T CAT over and over many times and did this for many words.

These are just a handful of strategies they used.

At home my mum was doing her best to help me with my English. Every night without fail she sat down with me. I remember clearly the many hours she helped me read green and blue Biff, Chip and Kipper books.

"Let's wait to see if the mother comes back," said Dad.

But the mother did not come back. So, in the end, Dad sent for help.

We did this night after night, and would go over the same books, but time and time again I would have forgotten every word in the book I had only read days before.

Looking back on it, I am so thankful and grateful for the help both my mum and Browns gave me. I hated it with a passion at the time but I know I wouldn't be the same without it. Even though it looked like my English was not improving, it built the foundation for who I am today. I will be forever grateful for what that school has done for me and what it has done for many others.

The teachers at Browns were absolutely amazing. I don't blame any of them for my learning at a snail's pace. They were very good, patient, caring and educated adults trying to make a difference. They just didn't know.

> *They didn't know that the 'WHY' I was learning*
> *was much more important than*
> *'HOW' I was learning.*

They didn't know that my own motivations and associations for learning mattered much more than 'HOW' I was learning. I did the best with what I had, and they did the best with what I had and I improved slowly. I will go into this in more detail later on.

As I said earlier, my first day at Browns was a struggle and I dragged the bad labels and beliefs about myself of being stupid, different, shy and awkward around with me all day. I had my head down and my shoulders were slumped all day. But through all the negativity Miss Kelly 'gave me a gift' she made me laugh. She helped me feel comfortable and happy. She made me feel like I belonged. Even if only just for one moment.

This one moment provided me with the crucial first building block to building my confidence.

But that was just one moment, one brick. For years at that

school I had no friends. My best friend was a wall because my favourite game that I played every day was 'wallball'. You guessed it? I would grab a football and kick it towards the wall, wait for it to bounce back and kick it again. I did this all playtime. Every playtime for two years straight.

What felt worse than 'wallball' was when my parents came to the school for Parents Evening. I knew they would see the truth. Me not playing with anyone and just playing 'wallball' all by myself. I knew even as a young kid all the pain my mum was going through because of all my difficulties so when she was finally happy that I was at Browns, I wanted to keep her happy. I used to go home and be so happy and excited about school. It wasn't a lie but I was still so shy and was dragging all my labels around with me.

However after each day at Browns there would sometimes be those magical moments like Miss Kelly making me laugh. Those moments that made me feel good about myself added one more brick to my wall of confidence.

After weeks, months and years had gone by my wall of confidence had grown tremendously. The big labels I used to believe about myself of being dumb, stupid, retarded, didn't seem so big any more. My wall was big enough for me to pluck up the courage to go and speak to other children and start playing with them.

After years and years my wall of confidence was so high that all my old labels seemed like nothing.

I became much more confident and I gained real friends that I still have today. I even began to enjoy school and sometimes I even would look forward to going school. I was developing the reputation of a class clown. I found that I enjoyed making people laugh so that became my main focus in class.

My wall of confidence got built because I was put in an environment where I felt normal. They made me feel like that my lack of ability in reading and writing was nothing to worry about. I was consistently being told that I could actually do it and being shown my strengths.

I wasn't pushed outside my comfort zone and was given work at my level so I could achieve things and feel successful.

All this gave me new experiences, which gave me new references to see and understand the world and myself. I pulled new meaning/labels about myself and believed different things about me. Things like:

With these new meanings and labels about myself, I changed what I believed I could and couldn't do.

The best thing about Browns School and most other special need schools is the supportive, caring, loving and most of all, the accepting environment the teachers and staff work so hard to create. Being in this environment, with others with similar abilities, helps get rid of the bad labels we and others attach to ourselves. They give you new bricks to slowly but surely build your wall of confidence and a more positive character.

In my experience, the teachers or adults who I

remember most are those that genuinely cared and took time to understand me. If they truly cared for me and wanted me to do well that's when I flourished and made most progress in English lessons and my self-esteem grew and grew. It didn't matter whether somebody had a qualification or not once they took time to get to know the real Theo, that's when I let my guard down and developed most academically and in confidence.

In my opinion, one negative factor of special need schools is the fact that all children with similar needs are in the same place. I was put with people who had the same difficulties as me so we all felt 'normal'. But we weren't 'normal'! We get a false sense of security about the real world and it does not get us ready to deal with people and situations in the real world.

Overtime I built a close group of friends and considered myself reasonably popular. But I slowly became bored of seeing the same people, having the same 6 classes each day, doing the same thing, day in day out. In the final 2 years I hit what was called my comfort zone. This was when I wasn't pushed or challenged. There was nothing changing me, nothing I didn't expect, and nothing that excited me anymore. To be honest I felt like I was drowning at this school. I needed and craved for something that would challenge me.

Because I had a massive increase in my confidence and built my wall of confidence so high I managed to get myself my first friend. At the time, according to my mum it gave me a new lease of life and pushed me to travel on my own for the real first time.

Browns served me well and I developed in many ways. It made me who I am today. They gave me something that is one hundred times more valuable than progress in English; they gave me hope and belief in myself.

I was desperate for a change of routine. At the end of Year 10, I accepted a place at Hadlow College for one day a week. It took me 2 hours to get there.

To get me further excited there was something new for me in Year 11, my GCSE's. I got incredibly focused. I worked harder than I ever had before. I took three GCSE's: Maths, Science and Art. I got a C in both Science and Maths. But let's say my Art didn't go so well, my drawing then and now still is not the best, not to mind my spacial awareness on a page. I also passed a functional skills test in English. This was incredible for me and I was so happy about it. In most people's eyes nothing compared to my cousin's 14 A-Star GCSE's but I was really proud of what I achieved.

This was the first time I achieved anything in school. It was the first time I proved to myself and others that I could do something. That I was clever enough and just as smart as other kids. I just needed to work harder and push myself. This built and strengthened my wall of confidence massively. Not in the sense of making friends and chatting to people but in a deeper more meaningful sense.

I now had enough self-confidence inside me to believe in myself.

The worse thing about dyslexia is not the inability to understand words and letters. It's the labels we put on ourselves because of our different learning ability. The labels of stupid, useless, retarded, the label that no one understands me. Thanks to Browns School who helped me remove these labels during the 8 years I spent with people who understood, respected and accepted me. Dyslexia is a condition and not a curse. I'm not stupid, I'm just different. Nothing worse, just different.

Looking back, Browns didn't come without limiting

beliefs. By the end of my schooling, I had a plan to go to college to study and then become a builder. I wanted to be a builder, because in my head it had the smallest amount of reading and writing of all the jobs I knew about even if I wasn't the best at DT. Fortunately, my mum saw past this idea and had a better one. She kept on pushing me to *go* to Frank Bruno's Boxing Academy, Orpington. After all her pushing I gave in and I thank god she did.

Chapter 7

The body and mind are connected.
A weak body = A weak mind,
A weak mind = A weak life.

If you can train and push your body to its limits then
you are training your brain to push itself.

When I was born I was born in the 90th percentile of health, which meant I was extremely big and extremely healthy. In all my health assessments I had as a child, I remember nearly each and every one of them being surprised at how healthy and strong I was as a little kid. My mum puts it down to having strong polish genes! Despite me being quarter polish I seem to have inherited more of the polish attributes than my brother. A lot of people ask me if I am polish. I don't know if this is because of my speech delay or because of the way I look, I think it's a bit of both.

Combining this fact with being a strong kinaesthetic learner, (person who learns through doing and touching not through reading and writing), over the years I noticed I would learn much more through doing and then through studying. I loved doing anything that involved my body and hated things that were fully classroom based. As a result of that and having good healthy polish genes, I loved sport and PE.

Growing up, I massively looked up to my older brother, Luke. Everything he got into I got into, everything he liked I liked. This is the main reason I started going to the gym. Luke went to the gym so I wanted to. I didn't have a clue what I was doing but at the age of 13 I was only thinking of getting abs and arms so that's what I did every time I went to the gym.

After about a month I saw some results! I liked what I

was beginning to see and got more and more intrigued and went to the gym more. Before long I was the only 14 year old kid that I knew with biceps and a six pack!

This gave my mum a great idea. She introduced me to boxing. I was interested but nervous to go as it was something new and never tried before. But I agreed to give it a go and she found Marvel Lanes Boxing Gym.

As my mum parked the car outside the gym, I could feel my heart racing. I was so scared. Once I got in there, it was packed with people changing their shoes, getting on their hand wraps and preparing for training.

A boxing trainer saw me and asked –

'Are you new?'

I said cautiously –

'Yes!'

He told me to go to Steve as he is the lead coach and pay him £3. I shyly walked across the room to Steve. Steve looked at me and said,

'You want to box?'

I nodded my head.

'You are in the right place he smiled. It will cost you £3 each session.'

After I paid and began walking away to get ready, Steve shouted –

'What's your name kid?'

'Th, Th, Th, Th, Alex, my name is Alex', I said.

I had a bad stutter and found it hard saying certain sounds and 'Th' was one of them and because I was scared that they would notice my stutter and make fun of me, I said my name was Alex because I had no problem saying that name.

I thought I was pretty fit with my abs and arms but that day I worked out harder than I ever had before. After a 30 min warmup of push-ups, squats, burpees and these things called 'bastards', (which is a burpee with a push-up in the middle), we then punched a bag, skipped and shadow boxed for one hour. After all that we then did a cool down. This in fact was the opposite of what it sounds like! It included doing pretty much the same exercises we did in the warmup but a lot more of them.

Through all of these exercises I kept thinking about what time it would finish.

Needless to say, I was back the next week to destroy my body again. I did this week after week even though this environment was completely different to anything else I'd been used to. I was still too shy to start a conversation with any one and they still knew me as Alex. What kept me going was one day my mum bought the full box set of the 6 rocky films. I love each and every one of those films; I guess I liked it because I saw myself in the films.

I saw myself as Rocky! I thought, if I just keep going day after day, I can become something.

As I progressed I got better and went two days a week, then three days and eventually I loved it and I started looking for fights. I had a couple. After 3 years at Marvel Lane boxing gym, I still found it hard to speak to certain people. It took me around 4 years to start to feel comfortable enough to speak to others. To this day they still know me as Alex! It was only when I moved to another boxing club, up in London Bridge, I told people my name was Theo and I felt comfortable to push myself to speak to others.

Mum:

He was the slowest English learner in the school. He still never remembered what he had practised the day before. He hardly progressed with reading books.

By age 12 he still couldn't pass the year 2 SATs English paper. But I started to take him boxing as a hobby that same year. Boxing and Theo were the perfect match as he was still large and in the 90th percentile, the Polish genes I think! He was heads above everyone else. Bit by bit he found his niche. He found he was good at something, he found he was strong and this made him feel good about himself.

After seven years of hard training, boxing taught me discipline, hard work, self-respect and respect for my coach. I learnt very quickly that if the coach tells you to do something, you do it. It taught me that I must push myself if I want to improve. I would say boxing gave me a strong foundation to build my character from.

When I have kids I will take them to an amateur boxing gym as soon as they are old enough. Not because I want them to box but because of the values they will gather to help them create a strong, admirable character and the lessons they will learn.

Chapter 8

Sometimes the worst time in your life, might just turn out to be the best time in your life.

Your struggles that you are going through now might be setting you up for something much better in your future.

Don't pre-judge it!

I wouldn't be the person who I'm proud to be today without my first year in 6th form.

It was now time for me to move school and start 6th form. I was so excited to go, I felt like it was my chance to be free from Browns. My chance to meet new people, create new friends and really express myself. I couldn't wait for it. I went to 6th form at the Priory school in the Frank Bruno's Boxing Academy department, like my mum had hoped. It included an actual boxing programme, a BTEC sport programme and a potential personal training qualification.

You know that feeling when you are so ready for something but when that something happens, you realise that you're not ready for it at all?

The feeling of excitement lasted for about three hours in 6th form.

We were about one third of the way through out first BTEC lesson and I quickly started to notice that I didn't have a clue what was going on. Then I remember thinking, I don't remember any of their names. I stated to feel a little worried. Everyone knew mine. I started to find it strangely hard to socialise with others. When I found out someone's name I would repeat it over and over again in my head. 'Peter, Peter, Peter!' But no less than 5 minutes later when I wanted to call their name my mind would go blank. The fear of them finding out I couldn't remember any of their names took over so I withdrew.

All my insecurities started flooding back. I remembered I had a stutter and speech impediment and remember thinking I didn't want them to make fun of me for the way I talked so I withdrew even more.

I started getting lost at school and realised that I still didn't know my way around the school. When I found myself in groups of people, I found it (and still do) really hard to keep track of the conversation and when I tried to join in, and say something that I was thinking about, it wouldn't be related to the topic at all. Then I felt even more awkward and embarrassed. I felt all the negative feelings once again. I felt lost and trapped.

Bear in mind I moved from a school that had no more than 30 children at its max, to a bigger school that had over 1,000 children and 200 sixth formers. I think it was inevitable I would feel like this again.

After a couple of months my head dropped again, my shoulders slumped, I started breathing more shallow. The feeling of shyness raised its ugly head once again and grew bigger and bigger each day, until I would go around school trying to avoid all the conversations I could. I felt a strong tightness in my throat and stomach every-time I was in groups and the attention was near or on me. I wouldn't speak to anyone at school all day. My mouth used to hurt because I never used to smile. I just wanted to go home and never go back there.

What had happened to me, I kept asking myself. I

At this point and time I was going through a very bad ending of my first long term relationship.

As you probably can imagine it sent me even lower down the spiral. It all added to my hunger to change.

went from a confident enthusiastic boy back into a sad, depressed and shy kid. It felt like I went full circle from having no confidence, from the start of browns to slowly gaining the confidence over a number of years, to then lose all my confidence after a couple of months at my new 6th form. It felt like I was back to the start of Browns (just in a different school). This is sadly what happened emotionally and physically. What had actually happened was my wall of confidence was built up by Browns School over many years, but it came crashing down after a couple of months of being at my 6th form.

This happened because I found myself in the deep end drowning in 6th form. I didn't have the safety net of Browns to fall into. I got forced outside my comfort zone into an environment that I didn't know. Because of the safeguarded view of the world I had experienced, it meant that I was not prepared for what was to come, so I suffered.

My view of the world tarnished and uncertain as well as my view of myself, I mentally withdrew back to my old self to when I started Browns because back then I didn't understand the world or myself. This made my wall of confidence crumble.

I HAD ENOUGH, I SNAPPED!

Chapter 9

'The only way to change your life is to take responsibility of your life. Responsibility = ownership.
To change anything in life you have to take responsibility for that change.
Whatever happens take responsibility!'

Tony Robbins

After some time, I made a decision that I was not going to live like this, that I couldn't live like this. I chose that I was not going to go to school every day and be miserable. I chose that I was not going to be sad, depressed and have crippling shyness. I chose to do something about it.

The only problem was that I was depressed and I didn't know how to change.

I decided to watch videos on YouTube on how to be more confident. I watched everything from strategies of imagining a confidence circle that I could step into and instantly be confident, all the way to videos of guys chatting up random girls on the street and getting their number!

I did this for months and all it did was make me more frustrated!

Then one wintry night, a storm was brewing right outside my window as I was watching my confidence videos like usual on my iPad. Just before I was going to turn it off for the night and go to bed I decided to watch one more video. This video had a big guy with massive teeth and a loud, dark croaky voice. I immediately thought this guy looks like he drinks because of his voice and red face, there's nothing I can learn from him and went to press the off button on my iPad. Just before I hit off he bellowed

'THE ONLY WAY TO CHANGE YOUR LIFE IS TO TAKE RESPONSIBILITY OF YOUR LIFE.'

My whole body was shaking as I listened to those words. For the first time I realised the reason for my crippling shyness and the reason I hated school, was not down to the fact that I had dyslexia. It was not that Browns didn't prepare me for the real world. It was that I was choosing to live like this.

I was the one who got me here!
And
I would be the only one to get me out of here, no one else.

This was the pivotal moment in my life when everything changed.
**It changed because
I started taking responsibility.**

For you to change, you must take responsibility.
Only you can change you.
Others can help but if you don't truly change your mind-set it will never be a lasting change.

From that moment on, I became obsessed with taking responsibility of my life. But who was this big teeth, croaky voiced individual I hear you asking. His name is Tony Robbins.

Not only has he changed my life but he has changed the life of millions. Lucky for all of us there are loads of free resources and videos at the press of a button.

I literally spent hundreds of hours watching speeches and videos by Tony and before long I was doing everything I could think of to improve myself.

I created a very long PowerPoint presentation (over 100 slides) of everything he talked about so I could go over and read it again and again.

I started waking up at 3am to do what he called 'The Hour of Power'. This is a morning ritual that I do. It's where I think of 3 things to be grateful for.

One example from years ago was - I'm so grateful for this amazing opportunity to shape my life the way I want to and create it the way I want it. I'm so grateful for having such an amazing, authentic mum and dad who went through hell and back to help me with my struggles. And thirdly I'm so grateful for my health, my body, the strength that I have.

I would not only think these things but feel them as well.

Then think about 3 things I want to happen and visualise them as done.

An example of this is: Automatically creating the habit of jumping out of bed and starting the day off right. Secondly, walking into school with confidence and thirdly attracting an amazing woman into my life. To this day I still follow the same format, and plan to for the rest of my life.

And lastly I would finish of with my incantations, not affirmations as Tony mentions in some of his videos. Incantations are where you use your body and your voice. For example, I used to say – 'Every day, in every way I'm getting more and more confident', over and over and express it with vivid hand and body movements for 30 minutes. I would imagine walking into class oozing with confidence as I was doing my incantations.

I was now completely obsessed. Focusing all my energy into trying to learn everything about myself, my mind, my body, how life works and success. I started studying and exercising at a whole new level.

I was learning everything about my own beliefs and values, understanding the cogs in my own brain that make me do the things I do, I was understanding all my own labels and why I had these labels about myself and what I could do to let them power and disempower me. I certainly understand everything about the body. I started listening to audio books about the body. The first was called 'The China Study', watching YouTube videos and trying my best to read books about the muscles and how the body functions.

I wanted to make the most out of my life so I wanted to understand how to be successful, I was listening to motivational videos on YouTube 24/7, I was listening to it when I was sleeping, when I was working out. When I was doing my computer work at school I would listen to it when the others would be listening to music. I didn't understand why others were not doing what I was doing. I believed that I had got my whole life ahead of me and I wanted to understand how life works so I could make the most out of it. There are many, many successful people out there saying how they got successful. I found it crazy that others my age (16) didn't want to listen to those people and instead decided to just wing it at life. I learnt about the power of state by Tony Robbins; how state controls everything. I started doing these incantations; walking up to my 6th form, saying to myself: I'm the most confident person in the school and imagine strolling to class in a confident way. I filled my bedroom wall with self-made posters of my goals, so I could wake up every day and look at them.

As you can imagine it worked. I felt a million times more confident and happier. I would chat to people more, stand up for myself and even started standing up for others. I took more chances and got better results in school.

One of my goals was to become a personal trainer and complete the level 2 and level 3 personal training qualifications. I remember it was coming to the date of the level 2 test. For this test I had to complete 50 multiple choice questions with only 4 questions allowed to be wrong, I put in a massive amount of work; spending hours at home reading and learning, my dad made flip cards, one side the question and the other side the answers. I spent hours working with the flip cards each day. I was using all my brakes, lunchtimes and free lessons working, struggling through it, and finding it incredibly hard to remember all the names of everything. After the test I was in a group of 3 kids out of 15 that passed the test. Everyone else failed, even some smart kids didn't get it.

I guess the first signs of me taking responsibility for my dyslexia were when I wanted to improve my speech. I wish I worked harder in those speech and language lessons in Browns because now I'm noticing that people don't fully understand me, people are still making fun of the way I sound and my stutter. I had the idea to pull out the papers with the sounds that the speech and language specialist worked on with me to teach myself. I used to say these words out loud every morning for 5 minutes and then I used to sing a song with phonic in from YouTube which was meant for 6 year olds. I also went to one to one every Wednesday with a lovely old lady, where we practiced these sounds over and over. It's amazing that in the couple of months of practicing by myself and with some extra help I improved my speech better than I ever had, despite my whole life so far having specialist help for me speaking and pronunciation of words. When I really wanted to improve, I did improve massively but when the help was handed to me I only improved marginally!

I felt incredible. People didn't know what hit them. They often asked me who are you and what did you do with Theo? Over time as I grew in the world of personal development I progressed into doing seminars. I went to all the free ones in London, meeting new people and learning more about different topics on how I could reach for the stars and realise my potential.

Chapter 10

*'Life is found in the dance
between your deepest desire and your greatest fear!'*
Tony Robbins

When you get face to face with your fear you can choose to run or fight. I chose to fight.

What's your biggest fear?
Do you choose to run or fight?

Life was going great. I had all these goals and was improving in leaps and bounds in boxing and with my personal development. Then it hit me!

One of the teachers, head of the Special Needs Department in 6th form said,

'Theo I know you don't want to hear this but at the start of next year you have to take English GCSE!'

I burst out laughing thinking she was joking. She added,

'Theo this is not a joke. You have to do it. We got away with you not taking your GCSE English this year.

I replied, 'You're kidding Miss!'

With a glowing smile she said, 'No! I think with the proper support and help you have a chance. Look how much you have grown in the last couple of months.'

I laughed again and said, 'Do you realise that I had the best help in England with my English for 8 straight years and if they couldn't help me how the hell do you think you can?'

I felt frustration and fear all at once.

'Well you have to do it. It's part of your curriculum,' she responded.

Over the coming weeks, I sat in English lessons bored out of my mind, frustrated and thinking I don't have time for this. I'm doing all my 6th form classes, boxing, my lifeguard job and all the personal development stuff. I didn't have time for English. Or so I thought! But it was just my fear of trying and failing again taking over and talking.

At this point I was under the stupid impression that learning English was not going to be part of my life anymore and that I would never have to sit in a dreadful English classroom again, EVER. I decided to disagree with Miss and stuck to my thinking of no more English lessons. They do say June born babies can be very stubborn! I stuck to my guns. My reasoning was that I was too busy. The biggest factor of all for me was that I had spent eight years of my life with the best help and education out there and still didn't get close to a C grade in my GCSEs. If they couldn't help me why did she think she could?

At this point I had improved every aspect of my life, apart from my English because I believed it was impossible. I thought I've already spent my whole life struggling and not getting anywhere with my English so why would I want to spend any more time on it. This was my excuse until one foggy cold morning, when I was walking my dogs doing my hour of power. I was feeling down on this particular day and thinking - I will never be able to pass my English. Then out of nowhere I heard this voice in my head say. What if? What if I could do it? What if I could pass my GCSE English? What if I could do something I thought was impossible my whole life? I mean, I've done all these other things, anything is possible, right? All the incantations, watching personal development videos and every morning doing my hour of power were paying off. I had transformed my mind-set.

At this point my eyes started to water. I burst out crying as I opened up to the possibility that this massive thing I let hang over my life and hold me back, was just me holding myself back. I was letting dyslexia use me and control my life.

Then I remembered what Tony Robbin's had said –

'The only way to change your life is to take responsibility of your life!'

And in that moment I made a decision! I made the decision that I was going to do whatever it took to get my C in English. I wanted to get a C in English no matter what it took.

I was scared. I didn't know how the hell I was going to do it but I knew that I was going to give it everything I had got.

Some of you might be thinking it can't be that hard. To me it reminded me of President Kennedy's speech about going to the moon. He and the whole country had no idea how they were going to get there. The parts they needed weren't even invented yet but they knew what they wanted and why they wanted it and were not going to let anything stop them getting there. There reasons were very strong but in a way pointless on the face of it. He said at the start of the speech – 'We want to go to the moon not because it is easy but because it is hard.' This made me ask myself – Why would I want to do anything that is hard?

One of the reasons I had, was to prove it was possible. Prove that it was possible for me to get a C. I wanted to be an example of what's possible and to prove I would not let anything stop me getting what I wanted. I wanted to prove being dyslexic would not stop me. I had the same motivation but just on a smaller scale. I was going to prove to myself and others that I was not going to let dyslexia stop me doing what I wanted to do and define me. I wanted to be a role model for others. I wanted to see what I could do if I put everything I had into it.

I started doing everything I could think of to improve

my English.

One of the things I did was get a little pocket notebook. Every time I typed a word wrong on the computer, it would come up with a little red scribble line underneath, and then I would speak the word I was trying to write into an App called 'Siri' on my phone. Siri would spell it out nice and correct and I would write that word into my notebook. These words were words I needed to learn. I called it the 'Screw Dyslexia Book' because I found it funny and I was going to screw my dyslexia up.

Back in those days, I travelled about a lot on trains and buses to go boxing, see my dad, go to school and see my mates. I often spent 3 hours on a train or bus. I spent that time writing in my 'Screw Dyslexia Book'. I used to write down all the words I got wrong over and over again saying the letters out loud till I knew the spelling off by heart.

Examples of some of my old 'Screw Dyslexia Books':

This is an example of me taking responsibility for my dyslexia, learning and progress in English and actively improving it. While in 6th form I managed to get one to one lessons with the head of English a couple times a week after school because of my persistent asking and my commitment to finding a way and never give up.

After spending hours each day on my 'Screw Dyslexia Book', sitting in as many English classes as they would allow me to and staying behind after school for at least an hour every day the results were starting to show. My spelling exploded and so did my understanding and comprehension when reading. I really began to believe in myself and that there was a chance that I actually had a shot at this.

Truthfully, every day was a struggle. Most days I didn't want to go into English but I reminded myself why I was doing it.

I constantly told myself –

This is for your future.

This is to prove to everyone that I wouldn't let dyslexia stop me and anything is possible.

Whenever I said this in my head it was go time. I would put behind all my fears and go for it.

There were many, many times I didn't believe I could do it. But I didn't let that stop me. I understood that it was fear. That it was a false belief about me. A negative label. That's why I pushed through the pain and pulled out my notebook every time I sat down on the train. I gave it my all in every English lesson and disciplined myself to stay behind after school.

It was not easy. It was not nice. But damn it was so worth it. Not because of the result of passing GCSE English but for getting myself to break through my barriers and massively improving my English. I didn't let dyslexia stop me.

> *I am an example to everyone else that dyslexia doesn't have to stop you. It didn't stop me! I proved that anything is possible if you set your mind to it.*

Towards the end of 6th form I was away doing a seminar in London. Slap bang in the middle of it my phone started to ring with no Caller ID. I thought that's strange so I quickly made a discreet exit and answered it. I didn't say anything at the start and then I recognised the voice as soon as she said –

'Good morning! It's Miss Solas from Harris Academy. Is this Theo Gough?'

'Errr yes… Hello Miss Solas. What's up?'

Stupidly not knowing why she was calling Miss Solas said -

'It's results day! Would you like to know your results for your GCSE English?'

As you can probably tell I had got caught up in everything else that I was doing that I had totally forgotten about results day. My heart began to race. I took a big gulp and said, 'Yes can you tell me them now Miss Solas please?'

She replied with a very happy tone in her voice –

'YOU'VE PASSED, YOU GOT YOUR C!

I was so happy and my voice shrieked with excitement that I had got a C. I had got a C even with my dyslexia.

I'm still so proud about that to this day. I went from having crippling shyness, being depressed and hating my life, to achieving so much more than I could ever have imagined. Most of all, I had a real understanding of how to improve and take responsibility of every aspect of my life.

I did this because I took massive actions. I didn't let anything stop me. I had massively compelling reasoning that drove me to break through my old labels.

I took responsibility of my dyslexia.

Chapter 11

*Realise that your so called disability is your greatest gift,
because it makes you who you are.
If you love yourself then you must love your so called
disability.*

Delighted though I was to get my English GCSE as it
helped build my character, the bigger gift came some
time later. In the early hours of the morning, when I was
doing my 'Hour of Power' and was out walking the dogs
at 3am, I started wondering why my life was so different
compared to my friends, and then I had a huge
breakthrough. I realised through a series of questions that
my life is so much different *because* I have dyslexia, not
despite it. My dyslexia has given me all my goals and
aspirations. I didn't get here *despite* my dyslexia; I got
here *because* of it. Every day from that point I have been
grateful for the fact that I have dyslexia. To this day I've
done incredible things that I never thought possible back
in Browns. I got my C in English, I've taught kids in
Nepal English who can read and write better than me,
I've read a speed reading book and now I can read faster
than my mum and dad, I am writing this book you are
reading in front of you because I believe the past does not
equal the future.

A month after my GCSE result, life began to settle down
again. All the well done's, I'm proud of you and good for
you from family and friends wore off. I kept up my hour
of power while walking the dogs. Life was great and then
to even make things better I was given the opportunity to
go to Nepal as a volunteer helper for 3 months. I passed
my personal training course so I could do my dream job.
Life was really going in the right direction for me and I

was so proud and thankful of what I had achieved and dreamed of what could be.

One day while doing my hour of power I asked myself why am I so different to my friends. Why was it that some of my friends and other people around me didn't have the same ambition and drive?

Thinking that yes they may be keener to go to parties and meet more people than me because I find it hard to talk to people. Then I thought about what is it that makes them long for Friday so it's the weekend but I can't wait to get home so I can work on my goals and dreams.

I was thinking that it may be because I got obsessed with personal development when I was at such a low point before I knew about Tony Robbins.

Then I started thinking about why I reached such a low point in the past and why did I find the hunger to change?

Looking back at my low point when I started 6th form, I felt so low because I had crippling shyness, I didn't have a clue what was going on in the classroom, I felt stupid and awkward and I got dumped from my first long term relationship. I knew these were the reasons why I reached this low point but questioned why I felt like this. I thought about it and decided that I felt shy, stupid and awkward because I had dyslexia.

That's when it hit me like a tonne of bricks. I started to shake and once again my eyes started to fill with water. I had the answer. I am where I am because of my dyslexia. It would never have clicked only for Tony Robins and his videos. If I never felt the need to change, I would never have had the hunger and drive to make the most out of my life. I didn't get where I am despite of my dyslexia, **I got here because of my dyslexia!**

From this moment on I can honestly tell you, with my hand on my heart, that every day I get up I'm so grateful that I have this gift called dyslexia in my life. I feel this so passionately it gets me emotional.

At this point in my life I have done so much more than I could ever have imagined and I owe it to my dyslexia.

To this day I have done things I could only have imagined back in Browns or even in 6th form.

I know I will continue to achieve bigger and better things, but for you to get full advantage of this book and anything in life you have to believe that the past does not equal the future. Without believing that simple truth that unfortunately so many people don't believe and go around thinking they can't do or achieve anything because they tried and failed in the past then you will never change and you will never grow. It does not matter what your so-called disability is, YOU CAN GET BETTER, YOU CAN IMPROVE.

The past does not equal the future!

Without a doubt the biggest gift dyslexia has given me is the undying passion to help others with dyslexia or others with any so-called disability. Teaching them what fundamentally changed my life.

The next two parts of my book goes into great detail about two overarching principles I used to transform my life into more than I could ever have imagined!

- The first principle is **taking responsibility.**

  Stop blaming others and realise only you can change you, no one else can. I'm going to teach you what it means to take responsibility of your life and you're so called 'disability'. Give you the toolbox and simple strategies to start taking responsibility.

- The second principle is realising that your so called disability is your **greatest gift**.

  Realising that you made it to where you are not despite of your so-called disability but because of it.

  I'm going to give you undeniable reasoning, logic and inspiration that you know and feel that dyslexia is a gift. That you believe this with your whole heart and every breath you take.

Part 2:

Take Responsibility.

Screw your Dyslexia!

Chapter 12

Step 1 - Decide to take responsibility of your dyslexia.

The only way to change your life is when you take responsibility for your life.
You have to take responsibility for your so-called disability for it to change.

You and only you have the _POWER_ to change, but only if you decide to.

Your destiny is shaped by your decisions. Decisions have the power to create you or destroy you; sometimes making no decision is a decision in itself.

*There are 2 fundamental **decisions** every one with dyslexia or any so-called disability make. These 2 **decisions** shape your life and shape the way you look at your so-called disability.*

The first **decision** is when you decide to use your so-called disability. This is where you take control of your dyslexia, you make the decision to not hold yourself back because of it but instead work with it, improve upon it, build yourself to be proud of it. This is where you focus more on improving yourself and making yourself better for the world around you. You take responsibility of your dyslexia.

The second **decision** is where you let your so called disability use you. You don't resist the struggles that dyslexia offer to you but instead you give in to them. You blame it on your dyslexia instead of on yourself. You focus on how unfair, unjust and cruel the world is. You put limits on yourself because of dyslexia, you believe it's impossible to improve, believe it's not worth it. You keep yourself caged by your beliefs about dyslexia. You never reach anywhere near your full potential.

These 2 *decisions* shape what you focus on, they shape what you believe in the world, they decide who your friends are and what sort of person you are going to become. *One decision* will make you see the light, will help you see the positives of your so-called disability and give you the belief to triumph over the struggle and live life to its fullest potential. The other *decision* will cripple you; it will limit your potential, and keep you trapped by your negative belief that distracts you from the truth.

These 2 fundamental *decisions* are the same no matter what your so-called disability is. This applies if you have dyslexia, dyspraxia, dyscalculia, ADHD, autism, a stutter, schizophrenia or even a health crisis, a death in the family, any fear you have and any other horrible, traumatising experiences.

It does not matter what your upbringing!

Whether your upbringing was supportive or negative, the fact remains; it's *your decisions* that ultimately determine the quality of your life. No matter what you have gone through, there is someone else who has had it worse and has overcome their difficulties and didn't let it stop them.

There is a massive contrast between people who have 'made it' and people who have 'failed':
- 35% of all dyslexics drop out of secondary

school.

- 40% of all juvenile delinquents (children committing crime) are dyslexic
- 70% of all children involved in drug and alcohol rehabilitation are dyslexic.

But yet

- 35% of all entrepreneurs are dyslexic.
- 40% of all self-made millionaires are dyslexic
- 50% Of all space engineers working for NASA are dyslexic.

Why?

2 decisions.
Use your so-called disability or let it use you.

Some may say this is a reflection of the education system not diagnosing them with dyslexia and meeting their needs, or it's the teachers' fault for blaming the child, its societies' fault for not recognising the differently-abled etc.

This may be true but what about all the successful people that got told they were dumb? Who got screwed over by the education system and made to feel like there is no hope? People like Richard Branson, Thomas Edison, Walt Disney and many, many more. What about them?

And on the other side, there are people who have been given everything - caring and loving parents, a great school that helped them and supported them, but now they are addicted to drugs and God knows what else.

The educational system, teachers, parents, society plays a role in what path you choose but... *they* *are not the determining factor.*

<u>The determining factor is YOU!</u>

You decide to use dyslexia, decide to take responsibility.
And not let your so-called disability use you.

You are reading this book which means you are one of the unique few who wants to take charge of their life, who wants to use their dyslexia and not let their dyslexia use them.

So make a decision right NOW. Decided once and for all that you will use your dyslexia and not let it use you. Decide to take responsibility of your own so-called disability.

From this point on this book I will teach you exactly how you can use your so-called disability. It will teach you the mind-set; tell you the secret of what really works, and why it hasn't been working until now. It will give you my very own strategies of how I improved my dyslexia but more importantly the exact mind-set I had, and it will give you the tools to transform your life.

AND MAYBE,

JUST MAYBE,

IT WILL SHOW YOU

AND MAKE YOU REALISE THAT

YOUR SO-CALLED DISABILITY

IS ACTUALLY YOUR GREATEST GIFT.

Chapter 13

If a child doesn't want to learn they won't!
If a child wants to learn badly enough they will learn no matter what.

In this chapter I will take you through the first steps in understanding the true power of your mind and how it's the only thing preventing you to learn in this day and age.

The mind is way more powerful than we can ever imagine. The limit of our potential is determined by our beliefs. With the right beliefs our potential is limitless. With the wrong beliefs our potential is halted or confined to a fraction of our full potential. This illustrates the power of our minds and our beliefs. I changed when my mind changed. I didn't change when I had more help; in fact I changed because I had less of it.

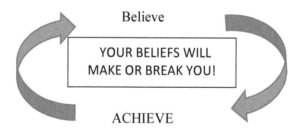

Believe

YOUR BELIEFS WILL
MAKE OR BREAK YOU!

ACHIEVE

If you are in a classroom trying to learn a subject, and know it's important, but have no strong interest in it but you have an incredible teacher who makes it interesting, relatable and enjoyable beyond your wildest imagination then you may end up more knowledgeable at the end of the lesson than at the start. However, if you have a mediocre or dare I say it bad teacher who doesn't excite you and instead makes the lesson look even more boring than you thought it would be then you would most likely walk out of that classroom not having learnt a single thing. This seems to be the dilemma in schools, trying to get incredible teachers not mediocre teachers.

But if you take responsibility for your learning then it does not matter if it's a legendary teacher or the most boring teacher in the world, you will have learnt more after walking out of that classroom at the end of the lesson than you would have known walking in.

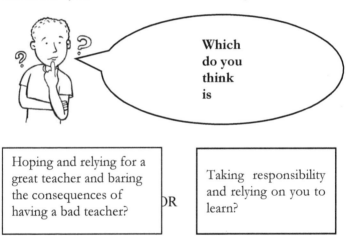

Which do you think is

Hoping and relying for a great teacher and baring the consequences of having a bad teacher?

OR

Taking responsibility and relying on you to learn?

It frustrates me, how little practical help there is out there in the education system, to prioritise developing someone's mind set and develop the key understanding of how psychology/mind-set of who they think they are and what they think they can do, matters way more than how or what they are learning.

In my experience of going through the education system, when teaching children who are dyslexic the first thing most professionals look at are the different strategies or techniques to use. What picture? What graph? What chart? Typically, for whatever reason, they do not look at what is going on inside the child's head. Whether the child really wants to learn English, or if they believe it's impossible and there is no point in trying. Whether they believe learning is important or they're just there because they are forced to and they are just looking at the clock waiting for the end of the lesson.

But you are not the educational system. You are probably not the teacher. You are most likely a student of some sort. What I have said here should not frustrate you but it should motivate you to take charge of the thing between your ears. I don't want you to agree with me. I want you to do something about it.

Stand up and say:

It does not matter what school, college or university I am part of, they will not be in charge of my education, **I will be.**

Take it from me, if a child doesn't want to learn, they won't learn or will learn very, very slowly.

I agree that strategies play a key role to achieving success. However, in my case for example, being dyslexic and learning English was not about the strategies of learning. They were the last thing that made a difference. First, my psychology for learning had to be in the right place and I believe this is the case for every individual, for every learner.

There is a big truth in life that people understand but never use. This fact is that:

> 'Doing anything in life is 80% psychology, 20% strategy.'
>
> Tony

To be able to learn, you have to actually want to learn and above all believe you can learn. For example, if you believe you can spell the word elephant then you will. But if you don't think it's necessary and, or don't believe you can learn to spell the word elephant, and then guess what? You won't! It doesn't matter what strategy you use to learn a word it will not be an effective long-lasting solution for learning English, (or learning anything for that matter), if you do not believe in yourself or what you are doing. Or even want to do it. When a strategy is being forced on a child to learn something they won't get anywhere near their best result or achieve what they are capable of unless their psychology is right.

If you believe you can and if you believe you can't, you're right!

This leads us to another challenge. How can you find out what you believe and more importantly how can you shift negative and destructive beliefs?

Now let me introduce you to the power of reason. When people asked me what changed for me to transform my English the way I did. I say one thing changed; **my reasons for learning**.

This is the key to learning anything. For anyone to learn something you must want to learn it. Strategies (the way you learn), are only maximised when you have compelling reasons to learn. Otherwise, if you're just going through information without a strong compelling reason for learning it, you will not learn and retain the information anywhere near the speed you are capable of or retain it for any period of time.

Having compelling reasons for something is especially hard when you have had a lot of pain in the past from that subject. Because from that pain there will luckily be negative beliefs or labels about yourself or that subject that put fake limits on your potential to learn and grow. Therefore having compelling reasons is essential to give you the fuel to push past your old beliefs and create new improved ones.

For me, learning English was a constant excruciating source of pain during my early years and as a teenager. I had all kinds of mental barriers and negative beliefs about anything to do with English or English lessons.

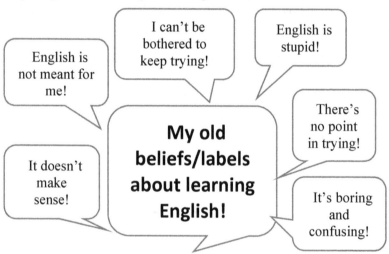

When my motivation was low, so were my results. I learnt at a snail's pace for 8 years at Browns' School even though I was receiving the best help in England.

However, in my first year in 6th form I improved my reading and writing ability over 500% more in one year having little or no help compared to the eight years of receiving the best help or support in the world.

Why? How?

It was all because I took responsibility of my learning and found strong and compelling reasons for improving my English. This change then led to my actions changing, and consequently, the results of my actions.

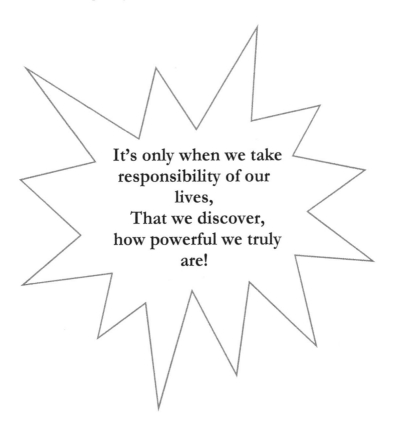

It's only when we take
responsibility of our
lives,
That we discover,
how powerful we truly
are!

Chapter 14

Step 3 - Own your dyslexia!

> # Words have no meaning!
>
> # The only meaning they have is the
> # meaning we give them.

Yes I have dyslexia, or can even label myself as dyslexic. In the Oxford Dictionary it states that dyslexia is:

> 'A general term for disorders that involve a difficulty in learning to read and write or interpret words, letters, and other symbols, but does not affect general intelligence.'

I have dyslexia but I will not let a dictionary or someone else tell me what it means to me or for me. I will not limit myself with the limitations other people have of dyslexia.

Years ago, I decided to create my own meaning of my own dyslexia. I decided I was going to find out what the meaning of my dyslexia is, and not let people tell me what I can and what I can't do.

Have you?

Have you let someone else tell you what you can and what you can't do because of some diagnosis and tests?

Have you accepted someone telling you what you can and can't do just because they say you have something called dyslexia?

I really hope not! You are so much better than that.

But if you have, this is your chance to create a new meaning of what dyslexia means to you.

When I got diagnosed with a severe and complex specific learning difficulty that comprised of:

- developmental dyslexia,
- a speech and language disorder,
- visuomotor difficulties and
- attention immaturities.

I didn't go around holding these diagnosis or labels accountable for my successes or failures in life. I don't say to people I can't do that or I find that hard because I've got ADHD, spatial awareness disorder and autism. No way! When the situation comes up that I have to write something down or read something I give it my best shot and if I'm struggling, I ask for help. I say I'm dyslexic instead of saying I can't read. But when I trip over something or can't find something, I don't say I've got a short term memory or I have spacial awareness problems, I just say I'm clumsy or I'm forgetful. This is an example of how I use labels in my own life but don't let them define me.

I'm not saying that labels are completely bad. I understand that they can be useful to 'label' people with similar problems into a group like dyslexic for example. One of the benefits of labels is that you can find common solutions that help people with the same label so that they can get the help they need. It also helps teachers, learning specialists, parents and other people to understand what an individual's difficulties are and what the best way to help them is.

If you have the diagnosis of something like dyslexia or ADHD you can't confine yourself to the limits of that disability, you can't let someone else tell you what you can and what you can't do. You're the one with the so-called disability not them. It only makes sense that you go out and find out for yourself what you can and can't do. We are all unique; we are all different, just like everyone else.

What I have figured out is that words or even labels have no meaning, the only meaning a word has is the meaning we give it. To me when I first heard or got diagnosed with dyslexia the word dyslexia had no meaning, it had no weight.

It is only when we attach meaning to a word then it has power. Think about it. Some people, like Richard Branson, can decide that dyslexia is a gift and use it to help others and some other people decide that dyslexia is a curse and put themselves in self-destruct mode. What I suggest to you is to take back the power of the meaning of dyslexia and start to define it for yourself.

Think about it with only you in the picture. Define it with your experiences and uncover the meaning of your very own dyslexia, your very own gift.

Think of the word dyslexia as an empty bucket that has no weight or meaning. It's your job to fill that bucket up with the meaning of what dyslexia actually means to you. It doesn't have to be called dyslexia and it does not have to be accurate, it just has to be a name that includes your difficulties. It needs to be your rock solid foundation of what your own dyslexia means to you.

When I reflect on my own dyslexia – I think about how I find reading and writing very confusing and in many ways a mystery that I'm still uncovering to this day. I find it easy and fascinating to understand concepts, ideas and people because I can create a visual image in my head so I see them in my head, but for the life of me I find it extremely hard to

Hey guys,
Let's play Hide &
Seek!

remember little details like names and lists.

For me objects are constantly playing 'Hide & Seek' with me!

I can put an object down and then 10 seconds later lose it completely for 10 minutes or even longer. This is always happening with my phone and car keys.

I can come up with ideas really fast but often struggle to communicate them with others because I speak too fast or my ideas become a little disjointed as I share them. These are some of the different ways dyslexia affects me! I know these are not all down to dyslexia; some of these are down to other diagnoses or being male!

According to some theories, but not all, my dyslexia is because of the mixed hemispherical dominance, which means the signals that are being sent to the right side of the brain sometimes get confused and send them to the left side and vice versa or another theory addresses the phonological problems due to cognitive deficit which is specific to phonology. The visual theory reflects the visual impairment giving rise to difficulties with the processing of letters and words on a page.

NONE OF THIS MATTERS!

As a dyslexic, I don't think they helped me in anyway understand myself better or progress academically or personally. In my opinion – 'Who the hell cares?' I don't care about what diagnoses I've got or what exactly is wrong with me, I just know what I have and who I am.

What I suggest to you is that you take full responsibility of the meaning of your so-called disability, and discover the true meaning of it for you. Go out and put it to the test and see for yourself what you can and what you can't do. I promise you that the meaning of your so-called disability is not the same as what people told you. You will find that it's much less a disability and something special that is unique to you.

DON'T
let
your
diagnoses
define
you!

I have a friend who was diagnosed with schizophrenia, because she could see and hear things that looked real but were not. This led to her taking strong medication to suppress what she calls 'her voices'. She is very smart and has read-up about schizophrenia, and knows all about what schizophrenics can and can't do.

Then out of what seemed nowhere her psychologist at the time gave her another test because a new study came out suggesting it may not be schizophrenia! It may be this other thing and that he would have to change the medication for it to be more effective. She read up about this new theory and had a new course of medication prescribed which hit her body hard and took a week or so for the drug to actually work.

However it was not long until there was another test. Another new bit of research that came out which of course meant she didn't have that diagnosis she has something else! And that required a new set of medication. This happened again and again with her for months. She had months of not knowing what exactly she had and what been the best way to treat it. When going through all these changes, changes of mood, changes of medication and not knowing what she had, there was just one thing that never changed; she never changed!

If you just strip away all the definitions of your diagnoses. If you choose to ignore all the dyslexia books, tapes and videos that are focused on what you can and what you can't do. If you chose to forget all of that nonsense and just focus on you then guess what, you might actually get somewhere. All you need to do is focus on what you can and can't do and work on making it better. This is you taking responsibility of your so called disability.

One cold December night in 2016, there was frost on all the cars outside. I started watching a powerful documentary, on YouTube, called The Dyslexia Myth. It's about Professor Joe Elliott saying there was no such thing as dyslexia. I found this intriguing and fascinating. His argument was that there is no scientifically, definitive way to distinguish a dyslexic from a non-dyslexic (a slow reader). One of the examples the documentary used to elaborate on his point was by introducing Keith Stanovich who is regarded by some as the world leading authority on reading. Keith thought like many of us that there is a difference between poor readers with high IQ (dyslexic) and just poor readers with low IQ, so he set out on a mission to scientifically prove this.

Here is some of what he said,

'Poor readers with moderate to low IQ, we gave the name 'garden variety' to mark the fact that no one thought that they were special. Dyslexia, which is reading difficulties combined with high IQs was thought to be unexpected and thereby had a special name. When we ran studies comparing dyslexics to garden variety poor readers they were startled to find that these two groups were virtually identical.'

After a whole decade of research, tests, and studies Keith decided there was no point in trying to divide poor readers into dyslexics and non-dyslexics because their problems were just the same. There is no real difference between dyslexics and garden variety (non-dyslexics that read at a low level). So if you give any child who is a poor reader a programme that you would give a dyslexic child, they would increase their English ability equally regardless of whether they are dyslexic or not.

And yet....

They only give the help to those who are diagnosed with dyslexia, which in my opinion is a huge injustice and a big flaw in our educational system.

'It doesn't matter if someone is dyslexic or not, if they need help and they can get help then they should have it!'

I got angry when I heard this and yelled at the screen.

I went on to think and still think it makes no difference if a child is dyslexic or not! Just because one kid has something saying he or she is dyslexic and the other child doesn't should never mean that only one child has the help they need. If they need it, they should have it.

The documentary continued with different people saying and proving that there is no difference between people who are low readers and dyslexics. So we could say dyslexia does not actually exist it only exists in our minds. Everyone who finds it hard to read is either dyslexic or not dyslexic.

This leads me onto my last point of this chapter.

Most children go undiagnosed and therefore

unlabelled with dyslexia so they diagnose themselves with being dumb or stupid which is infinitely more limiting. But I want to give you, give them a second choice. If you are reading or listening to this book it most likely means that there is something you are struggling with or cannot understand. If you think you are dyslexic or think you're anything else guess what I give you the permission to be that. Permission to be dyslexic or whatever you want to be. At the end of the day who cares if you are dyslexic or not. You are still you. I would still be me if I was not diagnosed with dyslexia. Dyslexia means nothing but the meaning or label we give it. It only means what you decide it to mean. This power comes with responsibility.

**If you label yourself with dyslexia
you must take on the responsibility
of creating your own meaning of that word.
You must fill up your own bucket.**

If we look at what Spider-Man's dad said to his son:
   'With great power comes great responsibility!'

What he should have said is:
   'With taking great responsibility you have great power.'

The rest of this book will teach you exactly how to take full responsibility of your new found so-called disability.
   It will teach you the power of meaning and labels and how they can control your life if you let them.
   It will tell you specifically what I did step by step but more importantly how I was thinking about my own dyslexia to make the shift.

Chapter 15

> **Step 4** - Uncovering your true so-called
> disability.

The worst thing about dyslexia isn't dyslexia itself but
the labels we put on ourselves because of our dyslexia.

The worst thing about being dyslexic is not the struggles we have with reading and writing. It is the labels that we or others put on ourselves and the limits we set on what we can or cannot do. All a label is, is a belief about ourselves, which can be positive, negative or neutral.

This chapter is about the controlling force in your life; beliefs. Beliefs have the power to create us or destroy us.

As mentioned in the previous chapter, most dyslexics go undiagnosed and instead label themselves as stupid, retarded, weird, or have negative feelings, like there is something wrong with them, which impacts on their mood or general behaviour. They can let this ruin their lives by putting limits on what they can or can't do.

You must watch the labels you put on yourself, because if negative they have the ability to destroy your gift of dyslexia. All a label is is a belief about you. If you think you are stupid then that becomes a belief. The belief grows and becomes a label of you. Your label becomes your identity and your identity becomes your reality. This then shows in your results and decisions. By calling yourself stupid, you can easily fall into a rapid decline and decide not to go to class, not to focus, not to try hard, not to go for the job or get that grade, and then guess what, you proved yourself right. You are in a downward spiral.

This is the success cycle. Don't you know people, who are always happy and seem to just get happier and happier, and don't you know people that are always sad and they find a way to get even sadder. This is because of the Success Cycle. That's why the rich get richer, the poor get poorer, the happy get happier, the sad get sadder.

The success cycle

First you have your **potential**. I think that the potential for anyone is limitless. Do you agree?

Second comes the **action**. The actions they take are directly linked to what they think they can achieve i.e. their potential, if they have high potential, they will take high actions but if their potential is low they will take little action.

Third is their result – the result is a direct reflection of the amount and quality of action. High actions, great result, low action bad result.

Fourth is their belief. If they have a great result, then it would change or reinforce their belief that they are a great and marvellous. On the other hand if they got a poor result they would believe they can't do it. They are not smart, they are dumb.

Your beliefs affect your potential.

This success cycle is the only reason I didn't change while at Browns, and it's the only reason why I changed in 6th form.

At Browns, I thought my potential for learning English was limited and dare I say it hopeless. So guess what, I took little action and we all know with little action, minimum work, not focusing in class; results were bad. I only improved my English millimetres each year. This reinforced my belief that I couldn't do English and I took even less action the next year.

However in 6th form everything changed. I started to believe my potential was limitless because Tony Robbins said it was and I believed him. Believing I had potential affected my actions. I took massive action, quality action which in turn affected my results. Quality focused action got me that C in GCSE English. Working on the spelling of words affected my belief about myself. I believed I could improve. I believed dyslexia would not stop me. I believed anything was and is possible.

This self-belief affects my actions every day, affects my results, and affects my potential. Today, right now, I'm sitting in David Lloyd writing this part of the book on my iPad with lots of red lines that I know I will have to correct later. But that will not stop me from achieving my potential, making the best life I can for me and all those around me.

Here is a screenshot of all the red lines and caption 2 is after some rereading and the use of Siri to help me improve it my potential:

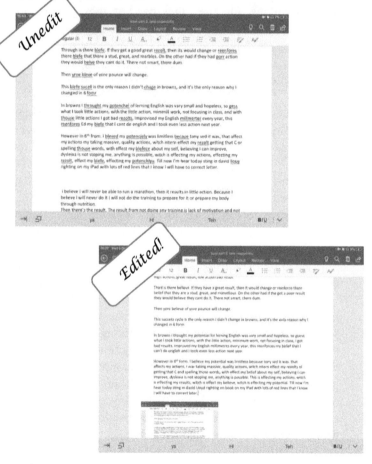

This also demonstrates how labels can affect your life both positively and negatively and why you must watch the labels/beliefs you put on yourself.

Jim Rohn taught me a simple principle.

Every day, stand guard at the door of your mind, and you alone decide what thoughts and beliefs you let into your life.

A real life example of how labels work is when I was in 6th form retaking my English. There was about half of us in the class retaking English. For some it wasn't even the first time they were retaking the class, for some it was the third or fourth time. I remember thinking:

If they can't pass then how can I? Their reading and writing is a million times better and some of them are quite smart.

In our Personal Training classes they would remember all the names of the muscles, fill out all the worksheets and get great marks in all the tests but when it came to the English they kept on failing. I was very confused until I started taking notice about what they used to say about English.

They were saying lots of negative things like:

When I heard them say this, I knew instantly why they couldn't pass. It was because they stuck the label on themselves.

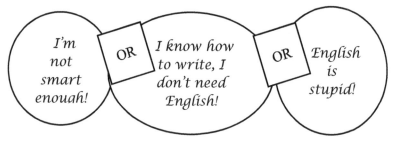

Their motivation or belief for passing English, which I think you would agree, was very weak and negative so learning was limited.

So guess what happened to these individuals? Yes, you guessed it. They didn't pass that time, or the next time or the time after that. Most of them left 6th form without a GCSE in English even though they could do the two fundamental skills of English, reading and writing, a million times better than me. However, I achieved because I believed I could and worked hard to achieve it.

I believed I could

So I did!

Below is a list of questions which by you answering will help you uncover your own beliefs and motivations for learning.

For this choose the subject that you are feeling in or that you hate the most. Then answer the same questions on a subject that you are succeeding in or your favourite subject.

<u>Questions</u>:

What do I say to my friends about
_____ (subject I am failing in)?

What do I say when talking to my parents about
_____(subject I am failing in)?

Is _____ (subject I am failing
in) worth my time?

Do I believe I can pass/get the required result
_____(subject I am failing in)?

If yes or no to the last question,
why?_____

_____

Answering these questions will uncover the positive and negative labels you have about your learning, the barriers behind your learning and the potential to understanding them.

Being aware of them is the first step in getting rid of all the bad labels in your life.

Compare the two lists, notice the difference.

If you simply swap the 2 answers it will transform your results

Questions:

What do I say to my friends about _____ (subject I am successful in and love)?

What do I say when talking to my parents about _____ (subject I am successful in and love)?

Is _____ (subject I am successful in and love) worth my time?

Do I believe I can pass/get the required result ____(subject I am successful in and love)?

If yes or no to the last question, why?_____

Chapter 16

The past does not equal the future. We hold the power to shape our life to whatever we want as long as we take control of what things mean.

In this chapter we are going to explore where our labels come from and why they have so much power in our lives and how we can take back that power and use it to direct our lives.

Labels are nothing but a belief about you.

A key question I want to address is:
Where do we get our labels and beliefs from?

When we are born, we are born with a blank slate. No religion, no racism, no beliefs and understanding of how the world works, we just have the innate instincts that every healthy human is born with.

Then we start to make sense of the world. Who's good, who's bad, what's you shouldn't do and what you should do. This model of the world is highly influenced by the people around us, like out parents, our siblings, our friends, our teachers, and the environments we are in, i.e at home, at school.

However, there comes a point when in childhood we become more self-aware and combined with a more complete understanding of how the world works, we start to realise that there are different beliefs, different values, different ways of thinking and behaving. We can choose what to believe, what things mean to us and what we want our life to be about. This is only possible if we take responsibility of our view of the world around us.

But how? How do we do that?

Tony Robbins says that we make 3 decisions every moment we are alive. These are:
- What has happened?
- What does this mean?
- What we are going to do.

I think it's the meaning we take from our experiences that shape our beliefs and labels which in turn change our lives.

All our beliefs in life come from this basic process:

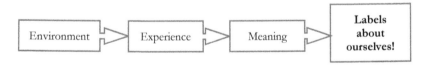

For example, when a dyslexic child is put in the *environment* of a typical English class where they are expected to read and write at a certain level like every other child, this creates the *experience* of not being able to read and write at the level they think they should be at and the surroundings expect them to be at.

The *meaning* they will pull from this experience is that they are stupid and dumb because they can't read and write at the same level as everyone else. They have

limited themselves by putting the labels of dumb and stupid on themselves.

We can take charge of this process. We can take back the power that controls our entire life.

We have this power but we must take full responsibility of this power so we can shape it to the way we want it. Look at all your labels from the questions you answered in a previous chapter and think carefully about how you decided to believe those answers or labels. The real power comes when we take responsibility of our own labels. It happens when we realise we ultimately created our limiting labels and beliefs about ourselves and it's up to us to get rid of them and destroy them.

You can't control the environment, and most of the time you can't control the situation **but you can always control the meaning you pull from the situation.** It's you that decides if you are dumb or stupid and it's you that ultimately puts the label on yourself.

99% of the labels we put on ourselves are down to the

environment we are in.

There is a reason why so many dyslexic people put negative labels and have negative beliefs about themselves.

Let's take a look at two individuals who had similar experiences but very different outcomes.

First we will look at Charlie's experience of school. Charlie attended a mainstream school and from the very beginning he noticed he was different. From his very first English lesson Charlie noticed that he didn't understand a lot of the content of the lessons and was not progressing anywhere near as fast as other children in the class. Keep in mind, the fact that he is in a system where it's expected that children read and write daily and if they don't then there is something wrong with them.

Charlie didn't understand why he was different, so he decided the only thing that made sense was that he was dumb. Here we can see labels raising their ugly head again. He thought he was stupid because he was not as clever as everyone else.

Charlie had two subjects that he loved and they were DT and Art. He loved being able to visualise something and then go off and create it from scratch.

However, after a few years of Charlie being terrified of the English classroom, being made to feel so different, so stupid, being bullied and made to feel left out of the class by his classmates he decided there was no point in doing D.T or Art for that matter. He lost all his passion and didn't even try because he thought he was dumb at that as well.

His negative labels and the environment he was constantly in kept drip feeding his labels. Which grew bigger and bigger every day. The negative feelings grew and grew, especially when the teacher regularly said to Charlie's parents,

'He just needs to focus a bit more. Charlie gets easily distracted and is lazy. If he just tried a bit harder then he would do better.'

Charlie built up lots and lots of negative labels about himself. He had firmly attached the labels of being to himself.

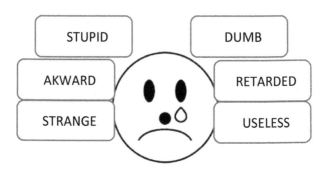

These were getting stronger and stronger every day.

This was only the beginning of Charlie's journey through school. He had only experienced nursery and primary school and already had these huge negative labels securely attached to himself.

When he moved into secondary school Charlie was desperate to find his place and see where he fitted in. When he thought about and looked for a group to belong to Charlie thought –

So he thought it must be

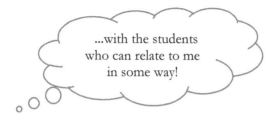

...with the students
who can relate to me
in some way!

That's when Charlie put himself into the wrong group and started rebelling against the system. He did this because he saw himself as a misfit.

By now, Charlie hated school more than ever before. He saw it as his enemy. Just like me, all those years ago, Charlie started acting up in class and became a mixture between the class clown and a bully. He did this to distract from his inability to progress or read as quick as everyone else and to stop anyone making fun of him.

By year 10, Charlie was introduced to drugs by one of his mates and he started using them to escape from his world. Escape from the massive fear of what he was going to do when he left school. Charlie got heavily addicted to drugs. His labels became more and more negative and he continued his massive downward spiral.

As you can tell from Charlie's childhood, our labels originate from our environment but this does not always have to be the case. The environment creates the situation and from the situation you create the meaning which is a belief or label about yourself. As I said at the beginning of this chapter you can't control the environment or the situation but you can always have control over what something means to you.

Remember, when you are in a situation where everyone is reading better than you, you can decide what that means to you. You can decide that you are dumb or stupid or different or all of these. Or you can decide that you are special and unique and that you have a gift doing something else and that you are going to find that something else.

Next, meet Charlotte, her story is very similar to Charlie's **apart** from a few little decisions about what she allowed her environment or experiences mean to her.

Charlotte started school when she was three and straight away noticed her differences even before she stepped into the classroom. She realised that she didn't pronounce some of her words the same as everyone else. She couldn't pronounce the sounds r, rh, or h correctly and often not at all. She also found it difficult to remember lists and names.

In Charlotte's first English lesson, letters and sounds made absolutely no sense and she hoped everyone else was having the same problems and felt the same as her. After a couple of weeks of English she was even more lost and what made it even worse was that other people were starting to understand it and even enjoy the lessons. Some even said it was their favourite lesson and they loved it.

At 5 years old she discovered Lego. She completely fell in love with it and was so fascinated by what she could create from these tiny little pieces of plastic. Daily she built houses and other great structures.

After her first term in Year 1, English lessons started

progressing at a much faster pace and she got even more confused. This is when she started daydreaming her time away in class and thinking about Lego all the time. She would think and plan what house she would build next. One time while in deep thought and planning mode about the different styles of roof she could add to her house, she got interrupted by her teacher asking her to read out loud.

Her heart began to race, her hands began to shake and her knees felt unstable as she stood up. She looked at the book she was pretending to read. All the words suddenly became blurry and fuzzy and started moving up and down. She stood there for what must have felt like an eternity.

Other children in the class started to giggle. Because of the extent of her nervousness Charlotte wet herself and the whole class erupted into hysterics, pointing and laughing at her. She started crying and did not stop for the whole day. That night she even cried herself to sleep.

She decided the meaning of this horrible situation was that she was different to everyone else. For her it meant she couldn't have friends because she couldn't trust them and they would just make fun of her. This meant that she hated school. This meant the children in her class would be horrible and call her names. This was because not that she thought she was dumb but just different. This meant she could never stand up in front of a crowd and read.

The day after she went to school and her whole class were calling her

'Stupid pee head' as her nickname. This nickname stuck for years and years.

She did everything she could do to get out of dreadful English lessons and most of the time she was successful. She hated every second at that school unless she was in the DT class. There she could express herself and her true character. In that class it didn't matter what people said to her because she knew that no one else could keep up with her in the class.

When she was 12 years old, she got sick and tired of going to English lessons where everyone bullied her and said she was dumb and stupid. She made the decision that the only way she would get through school without going crazy was by doing what she was good at, which was DT. So she kept her head down through all the English classes, through all the English tests and exams and spent every spare second thinking and creating in her mind.

Now,
20 years on, Charlotte is a
highly paid architect in
London and
one of the most highly
paid female architects in
the whole world.

Charlotte is now a highly paid architect with a growing family and Charlie is a drug addict and continues to this day on his downward spiral. Both had the same upbringing, both had the same gift for DT but one made better choices and most of all chose what the situations meant to them as an individual and what labels they decided to put on themselves.

One chose to take or use there so-called disability and the other chose to let their so-called disability use them.

CHARLIE   CHARLOTTE

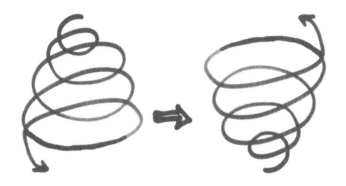

REMEMBER:

> **Environment** (no control) – **Situation** (little control) – **Meaning/label** - (absolute control).

For me, I experienced this with my best friend at Keston School. I was unruly. Always making trouble, not following the rules. You know that child that would be in the head teacher's office so often that you would build a strange bond with them. Well that was me and my best friend. We were just as bad as each other; we were the two trouble makers in the school.

However, he has now got himself kicked out of college, and has left multiple jobs and apprenticeships. When I left Keston I decided to make new, more informative decisions but my friend didn't do the same.

Take responsibility of your so called disability!

Chapter 17

Step 6 - Transform!

'Quality questions create a quality life.
Successful people ask better questions, and as a
result they get a better answer.'

Tony Robbins

The questions we ask determine the quality of our life.
The questions we ask ourselves control our focus which
affect the way we feel. Whatever question you ask, you
will get an answer. If you are always asking why me!
You will come up with answers. You will come up with
answers like:

I'm not good enough! | Everyone is better than me!

I'm not cut out for this!

However, if you ask how can I improve this and become
better, you will come up with a completely different set
of answers making you feel empowered instead of
disempowered.

In this chapter, we will strip away all your negative
labels/beliefs about your so called disability and discover
the truth of how you're so called disability is actually
affecting your life. You will see the truth first hand of

what is really stopping you. You will know the truth of how you're so called disability is affecting you in your life, clearly divided from all the negative labels that cloud your view of your so called disability. You will discover each and every belief/label you have about your so called disability and see them in daylight and know how this belief, this 'choice' is halting you in your life. You will see how low the glass ceiling of your labels is, and it will give you the power to break through the glass ceiling and reach your full potential in life.

For me and my beliefs of being dumb, stupid, different and awkward meant years ago that I couldn't get a GCSE in English. It meant that I would never be able to get a good job. It meant that I couldn't do anything that was reading and writing related so that meant in my head I could only become a builder. It stopped me doing what I really wanted to do and expressing myself.

This is what I faced when doing my GCSE English. I had the mind-set that no matter what help I could get there was nothing or no one that could make me pass or even complete a GCSE English exam. Of course this was just in my head. I had to break through all the barriers of my negative labels to be able to pass my English. This is why I can share this book. I broke away from what was stopping me. I broke away from my real disability and then I obviously passed my English GCSE. I even taught children in Nepal English and I have written this book you see in front of you. None of which seemed remotely possible when I had the labels of dumb and stupid in my head.

What could you do?

There are 3 fundamental questions I will ask you. However, it's up to you to get the most out of them. This is you taking responsibility of your so called disability because it's down to you to look inside yourself, look inside your mind with a non-judgemental view. I can only give you detail and description of what I want you to do, but it's down to you. It's down to you to take responsibility for answering these 3 fundamental questions about your so called disability as truly and honestly as you can.

With these questions you must be honest and state the answers in the positive and say how it's truly holding you back.

You must never use the words, I can't, and I will never, it stops me. Because if you are being truly honest with yourself, it's not stopping you, you just find it harder. Say it as it is. Not what you think it is. Say that you find it hard to read, not I can't read. When you see it for what it is, nothing more or nothing less, then it doesn't seem as big.

Question 1

Background Information:

My so-called disability is holding me back because I find it extremely hard to read and write at a good level, which slows me down. I get distracted easily. I find it very hard to socialise with others and I have difficulty with my speech or pronunciation of some words and find it hard to say certain sounds.

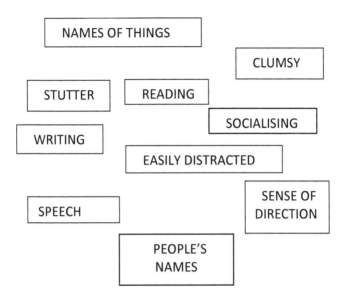

NAMES OF THINGS

CLUMSY

STUTTER   READING

SOCIALISING

WRITING

EASILY DISTRACTED

SPEECH

SENSE OF DIRECTION

PEOPLE'S NAMES

Some of these are slightly different or outside the general diagnosis of dyslexia but like I said before it's *my* dyslexia. It's NOT what other people say I have but it's what I know I have. I know what I find hard to do and I know what I can do easily.

This highlights the true reality of my so called disability and how it is holding me back. It highlights the true reality of what I can and can't do.

Again for me, my reading and writing was very poor, it has improved lots but still can improve more. My speech when stressed or rushed is poor but I know it can and above all I can improve it further. My socialising skills are bad, but if I work on them I can make them better and even be good at socialising.

The answers to these questions make me feel like anything is possible, it makes me feel that if I just work hard, find my own way of doing it, I can achieve anything. However, if I answered it according to my limiting labels I would say:

My so called disability is holding me back because I can't read and write anywhere near anyone else which stops me doing anything that involves reading and writing by myself. I am unable to focus for any length of time. I can't and will never be able to socialise with more than one person at a time. I sound stupid and never say the right words. I mispronounce my sounds all the time and mostly people do not understand me.

Answering the question like this will leave you feeling disempowered. If I answered the question like this then I would have let dyslexia use me and I would have resigned to its fate.

If you believe you can and if you believe you can't, you're right.

Your turn now! Are you ready?

The first question asks you to explore the REAL limitations and gifts your so-called disability gives you. It will be the raw truth of your so called disability. This question is not about your beliefs/labels or how it affects you but the facts of how it affects you.

Question 1.

My so called disability is real holding me back by

_____

_____

_____

_____

_____

_____

_____

_____

_____

_____

Question 2

Background Information:

The second question is designed to open up all the negative and positive beliefs you have about your so-called disability. It is with this question you will uncover what's really holding you back. This will be the key. It will open up the lies you are telling yourself; the lies that are stopping you from making the most of your life.

But first before you answer this question you have to know what your labels are and how you can search them out and find them. Just a reminder that your labels are nothing but a belief about yourself on what you can and can't do. In search of your labels you will have to do some digging into your mind to find out the truth.

There is one key question you can ask to find out your beliefs in any given situation by simply asking yourself this question.

What would I have to believe to make me feel this way?

For a hypothetical example: If I had been struggling in maths, hating everything about it. I would ask myself what would I have to believe to make me feel this way and my mind would say, it's because I am stupid at maths. This is my belief which in turn turns into a label I attach to myself.

In order for you to find out your beliefs you will have to know how your so called disability makes you feel. The best way to do this is by feeling a strong emotion towards your so called disability and asking yourself right then and there,

What would I have to believe to make me feel this way?

This will help you to uncover your beliefs but also it will change your focus which will make you feel better. So next time you feel angry, upset or any negative emotion a good question to ask yourself is,

What would I have to believe to make me feel this way?

For the purpose of this book I will ask you to think back over the last 3 months. Think about all the times you felt a strong feeling, strong emotion towards your so called disability and the difficulties it gives you – i.e. struggling to read, struggling to keep focused, people not understanding you.

As soon as you can remember a time you felt this emotion, write it down on paper, in this book preferably. Keep going till you have at least 5 strong emotions down. If you are struggling to find 5 strong emotions, go back further into your past until you find those strong emotions about your so called disability. If you remember feeling more than 5 then great, right as many as you want, just don't do any less than 5 strong emotions. Write next to the number, if there is any more, get creative.

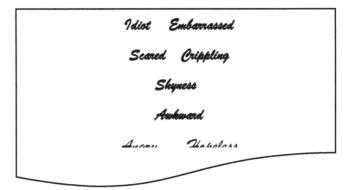

NOW GO, GO, GO!
You are not allowed to carry on unless you have done this!

Now it's time for the second step.
Grab the piece of paper with your emotions on it and then write next to it – What would I have to believe about my so called disability to make me feel _____ (strong emotion).

Example:
If I was to do this as if I just started my 6th form, it would be like this.

My strong emotions that I feel because of my so called disability:

1. Idiot!

What would I have to believe about my so called disability to make me feel like an idiot?

I would have to believe that I'm **stupid** and I can't learn like everyone else.

2. Embarrassed!

What would I have to believe about my so called disability to make me feel embarrassed?

I would have to believe that **I'm not as good as everyone else**, and that **other people are better than me** because they can read and write.

3. Scared!

What would I have to believe about my so called disability to make me feel scared?

I would have to believe that if other people find out I can't read and write, they would make fun of me because of it and call me **stupid**

4. Cripplingly shy!

What would I have to believe about my so called disability to make me feel cripplingly shy?

I would have to believe that I'm **different and retarded**, and if I do anything they would make fun of me.

4. Awkward!

What would I have to believe about my so called disability to make me feel awkward?

I would have to believe that **no one understands me** and that I always do **stupid** things.

5. Angry!

What would I have to believe about my so called disability to make me feel angry?

I would have to believe that the school doesn't **understand me**, feel it's **unfair**, feel that I shouldn't have to do English.

6. Hopeless!

What would I have to believe about my so called disability to make me feel hopeless?

I would have to believe that there is **nothing I can do**, that I can **never improve my English** and that it's a **losing battle** for me and it's not **worth my time.**

This list represents the real disability I had at the start of 6th form. These labels I unknowingly put on myself and carried some of them with me for years and years and they were the real reason I didn't learn. When I took responsibility of myself and what I believed about myself, I created this list of negative beliefs and realised this was limiting me.

> **Your turn!**

Question 2.
Part 1 - How I feel about my so called disability.

1. What would I have to believe about my so called disability to make me feel _____ (strong emotion)

I would have to believe that…

2. What would I have to believe about my so called disability to make me feel _____ (strong emotion)

I would have to believe that…

3. What would I have to believe about my so called disability to make me feel _____ (strong emotion)

I would have to believe that…

4. What would I have to believe about my so called disability to make me feel _____ (strong emotion)

I would have to believe that…

5. What would I have to believe about my so called disability to make me feel _____ (strong emotion)

I would have to believe that…

Now have you done what I asked?

You better have!

If you haven't go and do it <u>NOW!</u>

You will never gain full advantage of this book and never take full responsibility of your life unless you act NOW!

Question 3

<u>Background Information:</u>

To get rid of my negative beliefs, I did 2 fundamental things.

The first thing I did was easy.

I looked at all my beliefs. I wrote them down and I saw that some of them were stupid, not needed, and inaccurate. So I just decided to not believe them anymore and crossed them off the list, and underneath I wrote down what I chose to believe instead. It was as simple as that.

The second thing I did links directly to the third question.

The third question has the power to shift your beliefs from negative to positive.

But first I want to prime you. Prime your mind with a set of beliefs that will change the way you think about your own beliefs.

The first belief that you must install is that –
IT CAN CHANGE!
Your beliefs can change in a moment! Remember, you created them. Beliefs are only real in your mind and ultimately you have control of your mind if you so

choose. Believe that they can change in a moment!

The second belief is that **you and only you can change your beliefs.** You have to take responsibility of your beliefs. I can help you and direct you in this book but I can't do it for you and I can't be held accountable. You must hold yourself accountable.

The third belief is the belief that your negative beliefs **have to change NOW**! Believe that it's too painful to have these beliefs any longer in your life and you have to get rid of them now.

The third question is designed with what is called the pleasure and pain principle in mind. This was created by Freudian psychoanalysis and of course taught by Tony Robbins. The pain and pleasure principle states that there are 2 forces controlling all your actions:

Pain
Pleasure

Pain is everything you want to move away from and pleasure is what you want to move towards. This simply means if you have enough pain linked in your body to something or somebody then you will do whatever it takes to change and not believe that you have to take part in that behaviour or be with that person.

On the other hand if you link enough pleasure in your body to something, for example, behaviour, a belief, a person, you will do whatever it takes to believe that, to take part in that behaviour, be with that person.

This question is designed in a way to link enough pain towards your old beliefs and enough pleasure to not have those beliefs and creating new ones, more accurate and empowering ones. For this to work you have to take responsibility and link the pain yourself with its source. Unless you do this, it's useless.

However, this question is designed for you to see exactly how your labels/beliefs are stopping you and holding you back, see the limits it has already put in place, what it has stopped you doing. You will find out what you think you can't do because of these beliefs.

What you think you will never be able to do because of these beliefs. What this belief has stopped you doing in the past. And how this belief has ultimately held and continues to hold you back.

For the purpose of the book we will only be picking 2 of the most destructive beliefs you have. But I highly recommend you to do the whole list of beliefs somewhere else for you to get maximum benefit.

For me, the 2 most destructive, stupid beliefs I had were:

I'm stupid and **there is nothing I can do to improve myself.**

Example:

I believe I am stupid.

I think I can't do this because I'm stupid *(negative belief)*. I can't be myself in school; I can't say my opinion or say what I am thinking. I can't breathe in school. I can't be true to myself.

(Next, what you think you will never be able to do because of this belief). I will never be able to express myself, speak to people in a confident, normal way. I will never be able to achieve what I really want to achieve. I will never be able to be confident, speak to girls, enjoy my life; I will never be able to be normal. *(Next, what this belief has stopped you doing in the past).* It stopped me trying in all classes. It stopped me giving it my all

because I knew it would never work. It stopped me just trying the class. It stopped me speaking to other people. It stopped me making friends because I was scared they would find out that I was stupid and make fun of me. *(And finally, how this belief ultimately holds you back).* This ultimately held me back because I was never fully myself. It ultimately held me back because I thought I was a burden on the school, on my family, and society. It held me back because I believed I could never get good grades and get a good job. It held me back because I knew I was only giving one tenth of what I could actually give.

When you are writing your answers go into detail, it does not have to be perfect; it just has to be you. Don't judge your work. Whatever you think of, just write it down. Make sure you spend a good amount of time (no less than 10 minutes) on each belief. Feel the pain of keeping this belief. Make it so painful so you know you have to change, where you can't live with these beliefs any longer.

Then straight after, at the point where you feel like this has to change now, and then write down on a new piece of paper –

Instead of my old destructive, ugly, stupid belief, I choose to believe ….. (Create a new empowering belief).

My example:

My old, stupid, idiotic, destructive belief was that I'm stupid.

I immediately drew a line through the words and underneath it I wrote my new belief. **I'm as smart as I choose to be, as long as I work for it.**

This is what it looked like:

~~My old, stupid, idiotic, destructive belief was that I'm stupid.~~

My new belief is:
I'm as smart as I choose to be, as long as I work for it

I dare you to…..

- Imagine, to dream about what you could do when you get rid of your negative labels.
- Imagine the type of life you can live.
- Imagine what you will be able to do and create.

If you are reading this, or listening to this,

DO NOT SKIP THIS PART!

Grab a pen right now and bring it to the book. If you have an audiobook then write the questions down on paper or on your phone and then right down the answer underneath. It's so important that you take action and build on the momentum because if you don't you won't get anywhere near the full power of this book and break away from your negative labels.

Keep the answers close by and remember, this is you. These answers are your real so called disability, it's what is really holding you back and it's who you are becoming. Every time you feel down, every time you think the world is unfair and get frustrated that things are so much harder for you than everyone else go back to this and see who you really are and never let your labels or yourself limit you again.

NOW IT'S YOUR TURN.
JUST REMEMBER:

Question 3

My old, stupid, idiotic, destructive belief is

_____.

I can't do

_____because of this

belief.

I will never be able to

_____

_____because of this belief.

This belief has stopped me_____in the

past.

This belief has ultimately held me back because

_____.

MY OLD, STUPID, IDIOTIC, DESTRUCTIVE BELIEF WAS
THAT:

_____.

MY NEW EMPOWERING BELIEF IS:

_____.

Chapter 18

'Reasons come first!
Answers come second!'

Tony Robbins.

When someone asks me what changed for me to improve my English 500% in one year at 6th form compared to 8 years in a dyslexic school. I would without hesitation say, **one** thing changed. My **reasons** for learning English changed.

This chapter looks at the power of reasons and how they are key to unlocking the full power of our minds.

Back in Browns my reasons or motivations for learning were waiting for the class to end, waiting for school to end, waiting for lunch time, and endlessly mucking around trying not to get caught by the teacher.

Just to clarify, motivations are our reasons for doing something and in this case our reasons for learning. From my above behaviour, I'm sure it will come as no surprise to you that my reasons and motivations for learning were zero. I couldn't learn behaving like this; I didn't learn. Well I suppose I learnt something; ways to get away with playing the class clown and not catch my teacher's eye! But on a serious note, I learnt nothing and made no progress in English.

However, when I was in 6th form **my reasons** for learning English changed. They changed because I wanted to see what I could do if I gave it everything I'd got. I wanted to prove to myself and everyone else that I was not going to let dyslexia stop me from living the life that I wanted to. I decided I wanted to be a role-model for others all around the world to show what's possible.

I am living proof that with very severe dyslexia and other needs that if you motivate yourself and work hard the life you dream of or want is certainly possible.

I didn't use the excuse that there was no one helping me or who could help me. I decided to motivate myself and to help myself live the life I wanted to live. The world didn't change for me and it won't change for you, so I changed for the world and so must you. This gave me a bucket load of motivation to learn English. So I did.

A great man once said,

With strong enough reasons you can figure out the how to do it but the reasons are the key to unlocking the power of the mind, the power you have to achieve what you want.

Reasons come first and answers come second. It is because of reasons we went to the moon. When the decision was made to go, no one knew how we were going to get there but we knew why we wanted to go, so we would find a way to get there.

The power of **WHY** is one of the greatest powers that we have.

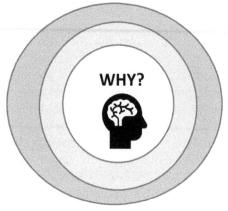

Your reasons **must** be strong enough to push you past all the hard times.

You **must** be strong enough to break through your old labels about your dyslexia or any other difficulty and make new ones.

If you don't have strong enough reasons to break past your limiting labels of yourself then you won't.

The reason you are not making progress in the area that you find most difficult is because your reasons for doing it are not strong enough or maybe not there at all.

It was my reasons that made me work extremely hard on my English, it was reasons that made me push past the pain of staying behind after school every day to work on my English, it was my reasons that made me pull out my dyslexia book every time my bum hit the seat of a bus or train and it was reasons that helped me deal with the frustration with the same words coming up time and time again in my dyslexia book. Oh how I hate the words *'because'* and *'exercises'* as I kept spelling them wrong! It was reasons that made me go to all the English classes and push past the boredom and confusion to learn. It was reasons that helped convince the head of English to help me one to one with my English.

Working this hard on my English made me have better results which gave me stronger beliefs about my English, which in turn affected my actions even more by cementing my belief I could do it and this sent me on an upward spiral. This is an example of the success cycle at work.

With
strong reasons
comes
strong focus.

There is something called the Law of Attraction.

In essence, the Law of Attraction states that whatever we focus on, you attract that into your life. If you focus on negative things you attract negative things into your life. If you focus on positive things you attract positive things into your life. I believe that you don't attract what you focus on but you get drawn to what you focus on in life. Let me explain more what I mean.

I think the Law of Attraction should be called the Law of Focus!

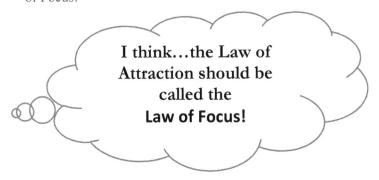

I think...the Law of Attraction should be called the Law of Focus!

My Law of Focus or 'Theo's Law of Focus' would state that whatever you focus on consistently you would get drawn to and anything that is related to that focus. When you focus on something you activate what is called your 'Reticula Activating System' or R.A.S. for short. Your R.A.S. is the part of your brain that tells you what to focus on and what to block out. It blocks out all the unnecessary stuff and keeps you focused on what is important. If you think about it, there are millions of things you can focus on right now. For example, your heartbeat, the air coming out of your nose, other people talking, your clothes touching your skin, the noise of cars going past. If your brain took all this in, you would go crazy. Therefore, your R.A.S. system helps you to focus on what is important and relevant to you at that particular time. Whatever you focus on you tend to notice more. For instance, when you want a certain car you may start to see that type of car a lot more. When you want to buy a house you start seeing more 'For Sale' signs. They may have been there before, but you didn't notice. Your R.A.S. blocked them out. But when it became more important to you, when you were looking for a house to buy, you saw these signs a lot more. When something is important to you, your R.A.S. pulls anything related to that into your focus. This is your brain's focusing system, and I trained mine to focus on learning how to spell and read words. You can do the same or focus on whatever is holding you back.

All you have to do to activate your R.A.S. is start to realise what you want. If you want to achieve a certain goal, focus on that one goal consistently. Create compelling reasons for achieving that goal. After you have done this your brain will be trained to bring anything related to that goal to your focus. Once you do this then you will find, new better ways of reaching your goal.

This is what I did. I first found all my reasons for learning. I made them so compelling that they would help me break through all my old negative labels of dyslexia and I focused intensely and that activated my R.A.S.

I would have never have got or started my 'Screw Dyslexia' book idea without activating my R.A.S. It got my mind so focused on improving my spelling of words that I started noticing patterns where I was spelling the same words right and the same words wrong. I put intense focus on the words I spelt wrong and took action to get out of the old patterns of spellings, and corrected them.

Now it's your turn to get unstoppable reasons that break through all your labels and have such intense focus that they activate your R.A.S.

Chapter 19

Step 8 - Create compelling goals.

'If you set goals and go after them with all your determination you can master your gift and this will take you places that will amaze you.'

Les Brown (Personal Development Speaker)

This chapter is about goal setting and the power of consistently setting goals. So far you have learnt that it's not your so called disability that's stopping you but it's the labels you hold about your so called disability that's really stopping and limiting you. You have found out where your labels you have put on yourself have come from and you have got rid and destroyed them while creating new empowering ones. This all sounds great and you have truly transformed.

But let me ask you a question, what's it all for? Is it so you can overcome your dyslexia and live your life to the highest standard possible? I hope so. However, you will have to know what living your life to the highest standard is, what does living your life to the highest standard look like? You will need a way to measure if you're getting there or if you're not making any progress. In other words you need a specific goal to head towards. You not only need a focus but a target - a bullseye to hit. Without this you will have done all this great stuff and broken past all your limitations but there will be no reason to use it. There is nothing to go for that pushes you and makes you grow. What happens to a muscle if it's not being worked? It gets weak! The same thing will happen to you. If you're not using what you have learnt, it will get weak and eventually and slowly your negative label about yourself will slowly creep back into your life. So let's not let that happen.

Think about it. All successful people in the world set goals. If you want to find an unsuccessful person, just look for a person who never sets goals and you will find one. If you want to look for a successful person, look for someone who sets goals on a daily basis, have strong reasons for getting these goals and regularly review your progress and change your approach to achieve these goals if you need to. You will see that most successful people in the world are constantly evaluating their performances.

Do you now think setting goals is important?

Let me tell you one more thing about setting goals! You are setting goals whether you like it or not, the question is if you are setting goals consciously or unconsciously. If you think you're not setting goals that means you are setting goals but unconsciously. You would set goals like - What am I going to have for dinner? How will I make it through until the end of the day? How will I get home after school or work? How will I get away with messing around in class without getting told off? All of these are goals, they are all things that you want, but are they low quality goals? Low quality goals mean that they have no real meaning or significance in your life.

On the other hand, high quality goals are goals that have

strong meaning and significance in your life. These goals will often be much harder to achieve. Goals like this could be - getting a C in English, writing a book about dyslexia, winning my next boxing match. These were my goals and when I achieved these goals I felt over the moon and they helped me in my life. However, getting home from school did not make me feel over the moon or develop me in anyway.

To make this clearer, let's look at a typical scenario. Let's say a guy says to me,

> *Theo, but my goal is challenging and compelling, I want to go out with that girl from school or from the office.*

Okay then, I ask him is his goal to go out with her for one date or to start a relationship with her? In other words I'm asking for a more specific goal. Because most of the time you are getting what you want you just don't know it because you are so general with what you are asking.

First, you need a clear specific goal. Secondly, I would ask him why he wants to go out with her. He would probably say something like; she is the most beautiful girl I have ever seen. She's smart and funny. I think she likes me and I really want to have….. Yep I understand what he's about to say. So he has strong reasons which make it a compelling goal.

You must have compelling goals. Next I would ask him about his plan of action. What is he doing to go on a date with her and he would probably say something like, I'm sending her messages, I'm speaking to her in class, I'm trying to make her laugh and feel comfortable.

It is very important you create an action plan. Then I would ask, if he is getting his desired goal by doing these actions.

In other words I'm asking you to review if what he is doing is working.

He would probably say - well maybe…. I don't know if she knows I like her and that I'm not just being friendly. Then I would say to him if what you are doing isn't working then you need to change your approach, change what you are doing to get on a date with her. What other things could you do to go out with her? I bet he would say, well, I guess I could ask her out for lunch the next time I see her.

This example illustrates the fundamentals to getting anything you want and desire in your life. These are the fundamentals of setting goals in the most effective way. There are 4 simple steps in getting anything you want. ANYTHING!

> **Step 1** – Have a specific goal.
> **Step 2** – Come up with compelling reasons to achieve that goal.
> **Step 3** – Take action towards achieving your goal.
> **Step 4** – Review, see if you're making progress towards you're goal and change your approach if you need to.
>
> Change what you are doing to achieve your goal.

Let me ask you something. If you are not achieving your goal after you've changed your approach, what will you do then? You will change your approach again, then what if that doesn't work, you change it again, and again, and again, and again, and again, you keep changing your approach till you find something that works and stick with that until you get your goal. Simple! But not easy!

The time has come
For you to
charge!

It's Your Turn!

Now it's your turn.

The **first step** is to choose a specific goal. Think of something that will challenge you and excite you. It can be whatever you want it to be. It could be, going on a date with that girl, getting that job or in my case it was getting that C in English. I would recommend for you to go for something that seems way out of your league, something so big, something so unrealistic, something that would completely change the way you think about yourself and who you are. At the end of the day it's not what we have achieved that counts, it's who we become in the process that counts. The best outcome of setting a goal is not actually getting the goal but it's what you become while pursuing that goal that matters.

Think about it! Choose one that you will achieve in the next year.

Write it down and be as specific as possible.

My goal is to ....

And I will complete it by ....

The **second** step, now the time has come, to come up with compelling reasons to get that goal. Remember the chapter about the power of reason – it's not how you learn it's why you are learning that counts! The power of reasons is incredible, with strong enough reasons you can do almost anything. So let's begin. I will lay out a series of questions to guide you finding the most powerful reasons for you. Remember, my goal was getting a C in GCSE English and my reasons were, I wanted to prove to myself and everyone else that I was not going to let my dyslexia stop me. I wanted to be an example for everyone else what is possible. I wanted to see what would happen if I gave it everything I got.

What are your reasons?

> The secret to come up with compelling reasons is to **make** it a must for you to achieve your goal.
> **Make** it so painful for yourself that if you don't achieve the goal, it will be agonising.
> **Make** achieving the goal a must for you.

TOP TIP!

Ask yourself:

What would it mean to me if I got this goal?

_____

_____

What else could I achieve in life if I got this goal?

_____

_____

How would it make me feel if I accomplished this goal?

_____

_____

What would it mean to my family if I fulfilled this goal?

_____

_____

What stories would I be able to tell because I achieved this goal?

_____

_____

What skills will I gain in the process?

_____

_____

Who will I become when I conquer my goal?

_____

_____

What are 5 strong and compelling reasons why I must achieve this goal?

_____

_____

_____

_____

_____

The **third step** is to focus on the goal obsessively in a positive way throughout each and every day. This step should come naturally after you get massively compelling goals. But when doing this you will come up with a plan to conquer your goals. Another way of putting it is to take massive action on achieving your goal. Do everything you can to work towards that goal. You must develop a plan of action, what are all the things you can do to achieve that goal, write down everything you can think of, every little and big action you can take and put that in. When you do this you will see that some of your actions will be more effective than others to achieve your goal.

What I would do is circle the action that will get you there the fastest with the least time and do those.

Complete the following to really focus and get started:

Now, I will do everything in my power to achieve my goal.

    I am going to…..

-
-
-
-
-
-

List here what you are going to do to conquer

133

Step 4 - Review. In this step you see if what you are doing is getting you towards your goal. And if what you are doing is not working, here is where you can change that, change your action plan again and again until you get your goal.

This step is arguably the most important and the most difficult step. It's the most important because it's the one that will guarantee success the most because you will keep changing your approach UNTIL you get your goal and it's the most difficult because it seems so easy to do but yet, that makes it so easy not to do, however it's not easy at all. This is because it involves being judgmental. When someone takes responsibility of their life, they have to hold themselves accountable for their life which means you have to be judgmental about yourself. This, I know can be hard and painful. You have to ask questions like, have I given it my all, am I underperforming, am I living up to my standards, and if you answer no to any of these questions, you will feel pain because you haven't done your best and you will need to improve. But it's this self-discipline of being judgmental of you and of getting a goal that separates the successful and the leaders from the rest.

For reviewing your goal you have to do 2 simple things. First, look at your specific goal and then ask yourself, are my actions getting me closer to my goal. If the answer is yes then great, hallelujah, but if the answer is no, that means you have to do the second thing. You have to change your action plan, whether it is doing more of what you are already doing or do something completely different. And if that doesn't work, change it, and if that doesn't, change it, AND if that doesn't work, change it, AND if that doesn't work... you get the idea.

Look at and review your goal weekly. The more often

you look at and review your goal the faster you will get the right action plan and the faster you get your goal. Personally I look at and review my goals daily.

This leads me onto my last point. My last point I learnt from my good friend, Tony Robbins. And it's about the idea of modelling or copying someone else who is already getting the result you want. There is no point trying to re-invent the wheel. Just look at others who have got what you want and just do what they did to get it and you will have it. Simple!

'Success leaves clues.
You can compress decades into days by
just simply moulding
what other people have done, and learning
from others.'
Tony Robbins

So if you want to get your goal as quickly as possible just look for someone who has already achieved your goal or similar. Find out what they have done and do that. You will get there much faster than if you do trial and error or go it alone.

Part 3

The Gift

of Dyslexia

Chapter 20

*Taking responsibility is about taking ownership of
your actions and the results of them.
It's not about blaming others for the way things are.*

or

*Blaming others for what has happened to you.
It's about doing something about it.*

This chapter is about Charlie, a dyslexic boy and his mum
Sarah going through the natural struggles and challenges
in life. It's in two parts. The first part is about how they
can flip the struggles on their head by taking
responsibility and the second part shows one of the many
gifts a dyslexic person has, **the gift of grit.**

PROGRESS
IS
IMPOSSIBLE
WITHOUT
CHANGE!

Part 1. The world won't change for you, you must change for the world.

When I was 17, I started working as a lifeguard at David Lloyd to earn a bit of extra money and to expose myself to what life was like working at a gym.

Very early on in my new job, I got chatting to a swimming teacher, called Sarah. It was at the end of her shift and we happened to start talking about dyslexia. It turned out that her son, Charlie, is severely dyslexic. I was so excited for him and said – 'Wow! That's so cool. How is he coping with having dyslexia?'

With a very proud mummy look on her face, she said really well and that she was so proud of where he was in life. Then her face changed a little; became more sad. She said that some people can be so nasty and horrible to him even when it's not his fault. Other people can be such a**holes. I was feeling for him and her. I knew what this felt like.

Then she told me that Charlie had recently started working as a lifeguard and he had come home a few days earlier, really upset at his boss.

What had happened?

His boss had asked him to clean the floor around the swimming pool thoroughly. He specifically asked Charlie to use a chemical based product to make sure it got a good deep clean and that everything he needed was in the cleaning cupboard.

He continued to say that there was 2 cleaning chemicals in there but check the labels carefully to make sure it's for tiles and you must not use the other one.

I knew what she was going to say next.

Sarah continued, getting visibly more and more upset. Charlie couldn't read the label on the bottles and didn't want to ask because he felt shy. He decided to guess and his luck had run out so he used the wrong one.

The next day his boss was furious. It turned out that the cleaning products he used are known to cause irritation and a rash when it comes into contact with human skin. All the people who went swimming that afternoon had rashes on their feet and as you can imagine the complaints started flooding in. His boss called him into his office and verbally assaulted him, he said -

'YOU IDIOT! YOU IDIOT! HOW STUPID ARE YOU? HOW COULD YOU NOT TELL THE DIFFERENCE BETWEEN TWO VERY DIFFERENT CLEANING PRODUCTS, WITH VERY DIFFERENT CHEMICALS? HOW HAVE YOU GOT THIS FAR IN LIFE? WHAT MORON WOULD OF HIRED A RETARD LIKE YOU?'

Charlie went home crying, he was saying how mean, horrible, nasty and inconsiderate his boss had being to him. After all, Charlie said at his interview that he had severe dyslexia. He was getting more and more frustrated saying that why is it always me doing the wrong thing and everyone else seems perfect...

Then she looked into my eyes and asked – 'How are they still allowed to treat people with a disability like this? This must change.'

139

Sarah then asked me:

What do you think about this

I replied:

His boss was right. He made a mistake and should be punished.

She was shocked. I could tell by her body language that she was not expecting that I would say that at all.

I then said that I meant it in a caring, loving and honest way, and that one of the things that I had learnt was …

…you can't wait for the world to change for you; you must change for the world.

**You must
stop blaming others
for your
so-called disability
and
take full ownership of it.**

As we took a seat and chatted some more I talked to her further about Charlie taking responsibility for his dyslexia. I explained to her that her son had two ways of dealing with the situation.

The **first way** was by blaming others, his boss in this case, and saying the boss was mean, nasty and a terrible boss. And that he should have helped him and pointed out what words or names of chemicals on the products to look for. Putting all the responsibility and blame on his boss just because he knew he had dyslexia.

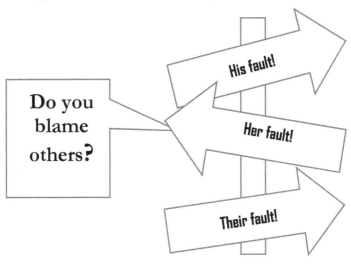

Or the **second way**. He could take the telling off for what it was and realise that he did use the wrong chemicals and that people did get a rash on their feet all because he had taken a chance and used the wrong products. It was because of him the swimmers had developed a rash. He could learn from this experience and realise he needed to find a way to make sure something like that did not happen again. The next time he should ask someone to check he had got the right cleaning products or explain to his boss he was not sure which to use and ask his boss what colour or to show him which one. From here he could try his best to remember it.

Do you Learn from your experiences?

I cannot stress enough the importance of the above story. This is just one example but this happens so often in our lives, dyslexic or not. When we get blamed for something, don't do what we said we would do, or in simpler words fail we decide to blame everyone else and say it's their fault. But, we can decide to take responsibility and decide that it is our own fault and do something about it. They won't change, only you can!

We will now take Charlie's story and focus on the two ways he could have dealt with what happened and use it as a learning tool.

The first way of dealing with the situation will not work for long. It will only keep working until the next mistake happens and then what? Carry on blaming others? Blame others because they didn't help you?

Will you do this again and again? Keep doing it until you hate the whole world? Continue until you hate your dyslexia even more? If you let dyslexia use you, if you let it control your whole life then you will end up in the dysfunctional category (chapter 12).

The second way is the winning way and is where you take responsibility of your so called disability. You realise that when you make a mistake that you need to change and do something to make sure that you minimise the chances of it happening again or hopefully never happening again.

Over time you design coping strategies and a skill set to help you.

You could...

- ask people to help you,
- take photos of something to remind you what to use,
- ask for visuals to help you know what something looks like,
- find a way around your so-called disability so the same situation does not happen again.

This is where you are using your dyslexia and you're not letting it use you. People, who take responsibility and use the gift of grit, end up in the successful category of dyslexics (chapter 12).

After our conversation, Sarah realised and agreed that the world couldn't or wouldn't change for her son and her son would have to change for the world if he was going to be happy and successful. She shared my idea with her son and stressed to him that he needed to change for the world and really take responsibility for his dyslexia.

Part 2. The Gift of Grit.

Every time I saw Sarah I would ask about Charlie. After a few months when we were chatting again I noticed her smile was beaming from ear to ear and she was so positive.

I am so proud of Charlie. How hard he is working, and how he has put his head down and pushed through school and now he is at university studying archaeology. I am amazed at how hard he is working and has worked even though he has dyslexia. And, guess what...other students in his class have dyslexia and work hard just like him.

I said to her.

... That's so great, but you realise that he didn't go to university and is studying archaeology despite his dyslexia but he is doing it all because of it.

*People who have dyslexia have an amazing ability to visualise what they want to create and move their mental image around in their head. That's why he chose archaeology, and that's why he will be amazing at it. Of course he works hard, it's because he have dyslexia, because he had to develop the mental strength over time to work hard and to push himself through the hard times. This is what I call the '***gift of grit.***' And that is exactly what, Charlie, had done.*

Sarah then shared with me that when her husband past

144

away that her son and older daughter dealt with it completely differently. Charlie had hid himself away in his room for a whole year and channelled his emotion into his studies and schoolwork. He flourished at school and everyone was amazed at how well he was doing.

But Caroline (her daughter), dealt with the situation completely differently. Her personality changed and she started getting very, very angry. She kept getting into trouble at school and was sent home from school multiple times for getting into fights. She changed her friendship group and started hanging out with the wrong crowd. She started coming home later and later and sometimes not come home at all. She had even found drugs in her room a number of times and school was non-existent.

Then Sarah asked in a very emotionally caring way –

> *Has this got anything to do with dyslexia?*

I said:

> *This has everything to do with dyslexia. The reasons Charlie dealt with the situation so differently is because he has the gift of grit. Your son has had to deal with so much going through school, and was going through so many challenges and obstacles because of his dyslexia, that he had to find solutions to deal with it and now because of it he has developed coping mechanisms and was able to channel his emotions from his dad's death into his studying.*
>
> *But your daughter who does not have dyslexia has not had the same struggles in her life so she hadn't developed the right coping mechanisms that work for her and therefore was unable to cope with her dad's death in a way that didn't destroy her life.*

145

This is a perfect example of the **gift of grit** at work and growing up with dyslexia is the perfect opportunity to grow this skill.

Do you know anyone who has had every opportunity in life, someone who has had a great upbringing, is very smart and intelligent but yet are really struggling, and can't stand on their own two feet?

You often see other people who have been through so much, have had a bad upbringing but yet have a much better quality of life and are doing much better than people who had everything handed to them on a plate.

This is because the one who had everything didn't have any real struggle, they have no 'emotional muscle' so they can't deal with the hard times as they journey through life. But the people who have been through hell and back have grown emotional muscle, so that when something bad happens in their life they have strategies to help them deal with it emotionally. This is what 'emotional muscle' is, you can deal with it a lot more than others who had it easier than you.

I have always said I feel sorry for the person who finds school and life a gentle breeze because they have not developed emotional muscle or a skill set to help them overcome obstacles or push themselves to go for what they really want.

Because of my schooling and having to work ten times harder than most others to be at the same level, I'm used to pushing myself mentally and physically. If I hadn't I wouldn't have the resilience to write and above all finish this book. If you are not used to pushing yourself you will never go out of your comfort zone to do things to make you grow.

Without developing the 'gift of grit' at a young age I would never have achieved what I have or become the man I am today.

When I was sitting in an English lesson, in my old mainstream school, I was always waiting for the time to pass, hoping and praying that the teacher wouldn't notice that I hadn't written a single word in my book. The only subject that I could stand my own was in maths. In reality I was in the bottom group of the class but it was the only lesson I could understand. I felt at the time that I was the best in the class so that's why I was so focused on improving it. I decided to put every effort into each lesson and task set.

Over the years, thinking I was the best in the class and trying my absolute best in every lesson because I thought I was good at it, helped me enjoy it and it made me feel happier about myself, it made me feel 'normal'. Overtime and through hard work and focus, I slowly rose to the top group in the class. This was fully because of my effort, not my ability. It was my effort that was the key to my success at that time.

When I was 8, I didn't know how hard the other children were working in comparison; I just thought we were all working as hard as each other. This is how I saw and approached life because of the gift of grit.

Another example from my life was when I was studying for my Level Two Personal Training qualification. There was a big theory test I had to pass to gain my qualification. This was made up of 50 multiple choice questions and I had to get 45 or above to pass. I knew this was the one thing I wanted to do and I had to get this so I dedicated every free hour I had at school going through all the mock papers and worked my way through hundreds of examples. I spent hours each day at home going through them. Everyone in the class thought of me as the dumb one, the one who did not speak, the one who couldn't answer the questions and did not focus in lessons.

I was the one everyone least expected to pass. But, I was one of the three who passed out of 15. The three of us really wanted it and achieved it through pure hard work or 'grit'.

Our brain works in a very similar way to the muscles in our body. They both get stronger and more effective with use.

How does the gift of grit work?

One of my first clients as a personal trainer is a classic example of this. She believed that she could never do a full push-up! However, when she started training she began to get stronger, she lost weight and began doing half push ups on her knees directly under her hips. And as she trained more and got stronger she could do a full push up with her knees on the floor under her hips. Slowly, she moved her knees further and further away from her which put more weight on her arms that she needed to press from, and the more she practised, the stronger she got and her push ups got deeper and deeper.

Now 9 months from day 1 she can do 10 full push ups

without her knees touching the ground. To do this I gave her one piece of advice - every day do 30 push ups. And each day she did, she got stronger over time.

When we don't use our muscles they become weak and when we use our muscles then we get stronger and overtime what used to be hard gets easier. Our emotional muscles work the same way. If we have never worked hard and never used discipline then the first day we have to will be extremely hard. But if we have been working hard and using discipline for years and years then one more day of using them won't feel like hard work, it will just feel like another day. This doesn't just go for working hard and discipline; this is the same with happiness, being grateful, being passionate and being driven. The more we use these, the more we have of them to use.

As the saying goes –

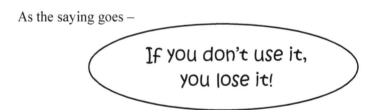

If you don't use it, you lose it!

This is the same for negative emotions. The more we use them, the stronger and the easier it is to feel those emotions. I can write a whole book about this subject but in this case I am just using it to illustrate how the gift of grit works.

What I have found is that most dyslexics do well in a subject like maths, science or DT. The gift of grit is developed through struggles. It is important that you understand that grit is the same as having strong discipline and a good work ethic. These can be seen as 'emotional muscles' and they can be strengthened when they are used and weakened when they are neglected. This is the same as with your physical muscles. To grow your physical muscles you need to go to the gym, a class or train and use them. What happens when you sit on your ass all day and don't use your muscles? You get weaker and weaker. This is the same for your emotional muscles and if you have never worked a day in your life and then the first day you do work it will exhaust you, but if you have been working hard for 10 years, one more day won't kill you.

Do you understand what I'm trying to say?

Every time you are in that English lesson and trying extremely hard, using all your focus, trying to read, and then you go into a maths lesson and use the same focus and work ethic which is ten times more than everyone else, over time you will get better than the others because the more you put into the lesson the more you will get out of it. Over years of struggling with English lessons you will develop a hard skin and a hard work ethic will become natural to you without you even noticing.

This is called
the
gift of grit.

Grit
(noun)
courage, bravery, pluck, mettle, backbone, spirit, strength of character, strength of will, moral fibre, steel, nerve, fortitude, toughness, hardiness, resolve, resolution, determination, perseverance, endurance, informal, guts, spunk.

If you blame your dyslexia for all the rubbish in your life then you better blame it for all the good too. Yes, I do blame my dyslexia for the fact I find reading and spelling very hard and struggle to keep up with everyone else.

Never, ever, say that dyslexia is only a negative!
If you blame your dyslexia for all the bad, you must
blame it for all the good as well.

But, more importantly I also blame my dyslexia for my insatiable hunger to get the most out of my life. I blame my dyslexia for my amazing and unique ability to imagine things in great detail and to understand complex concepts. I blame my dyslexia for my unstoppable passion to help everyone else with dyslexia and tell them the truth about what's stopping them. All of this comes from the fact that I have dyslexia.

This is how you will discover and really believe that dyslexia is a gift in your life.

Ask yourself these two questions and give yourself time to answer each of them in turn.

Q1. What negative things do I blame dyslexia for?

Q2. What positive things can I blame dyslexia for?

Chapter 21

F**K dyslexia!
I decided I was going to f**k my dyslexia up.

In previous chapters, we have discussed your reasons and how your 'want' for learning is much more important than how you are learning.

REASONS COME FIRST,

AND

ANSWERS COME SECOND!

This can apply to any subject, any area of your life that you are struggling in, or to something you have told yourself you can't do, for example, doing a press-up.

This chapter focuses on the strategy for how I improved my English 500% in one year compared to 8 years having all the help I could ever want. It's about everything I did, how I did it and how much I did it.

The reason behind calling this chapter 'F**K Dyslexia' is because I decided I was going to 'f**K' or not let my dyslexia rule my life! I was going to destroy the status quo around that I'd been living all my life. The status quo that had me thinking and believing dyslexia was what was stopping me doing things I wanted to do. My dyslexia was going to take a back seat and I was going to be the driving force in my life. I was going to steer my life down the path I decided and not by my dyslexia or by what others wanted from me.

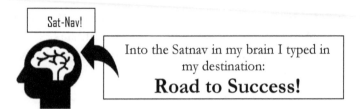

Sat-Nav!

Into the Satnav in my brain I typed in my destination:
Road to Success!

I decided I was going to work so hard and learn to spell the words I had never been able to spell before.

I wanted to become fluent in my writing, and be able to read anything I wanted to.

On a wet Wednesday evening in May 2016 around 4pm, shortly after I made the decision that I was going to improve my English, an idea came to me. I was already staying after school correcting the spelling of my BETEC Sport coursework using an app called Siri on my phone to spell words correctly, and then writing them correctly on the computer. An idea came to me. I immediately stopped what I was doing and picked up my phone to call my mum to ask her if she had a little notebook that I could use.

I now had my own idea of how to correct all the words I was spelling wrong. This really filled me with pride. The enthusiasm that was pushing me to take responsibility was now developing rapidly and I was developing my own ways to progress. A way that nobody else shared with me and I knew it would work.

The process I used was:

Figure out the misspelt words by looking for red lines under them in my coursework on the computer.

Find the correct spelling for these words on my phone

using Siri.

Write the correct spelling of the word in my little notebook.

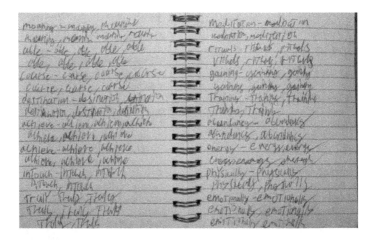

As a result, I had a little notebook full of words that I needed to learn how to spell. The final step to learn how to spell these words was simple. I would re-write these words again and again until they were absorbed in my brain. Et voila! I would know the correct spelling of the word without trying when I needed to use it again. I then named the notebook 'Screw Dyslexia'. This made me laugh, and laugh, and laugh. It was so funny and exciting to me that I had figured out a way that I was going to screw my dyslexia and finally learn English.

From that day on, I continued to stay after school every day for an extra hour (at least). Every word I misspelt as I typed away my coursework on the computer I wrote into this book. Bear in mind, when I started actively working on my spelling, I got an average of one word wrong in every three.

Example:

> We hav a range of Musels in oure body.

Imagine how many times this book got used and how often it got filled up.

Every time I was on the bus, train, tram, anywhere I would pull the book out and practise the words I had written in. I would write each word three times.

Then, I remembered some of the strategies I learnt at Browns. Another epiphany! I could use these to help me improve further.

The strategies were:

1. I started saying the letters of the word over and over again. For example, if I wanted to learn the word cat, I would say out loud the letters: C A T and then say the word afterwards: cat, C A T cat, C A T cat. I also did this three times. I used to do this with each word over and over again and as I repeated it, I got faster and faster each time, until I memorised the letters without having to look at the word.

2. Also, I tried imagining the letter in my head as I was saying each letter, and the word when I was finished. I would imagine them burning a bright red fiery colour, each time burning brighter and brighter until it felt like it was permanently burnt into my brain like a tattoo.

3. A third strategy I used was writing the letters out with my finger in the air as I was saying them. For example, when saying cat, I would spell C A T in the air with my finger at the same time. I would write the word in the air with my finger over and over again, getting faster and faster, to the point where it felt like there was smoke coming out of my fingers. When I got up to what felt like the max speed, I would then immediately explode that word; writing it down in my 'Screw Dyslexia' book, writing it around 5 to 10 times. It took about 1 minute for one word. My goal was to stick in a new pattern of spelling of a word in my head and kick the old incorrect pattern of spelling out.

When writing in my spelling book, I had three rules.

I would not write the word down on paper unless I knew the letters of that word off by heart at that moment. I was not allowed to look at the word anywhere as I was writing it down on paper. If I forgot how to spell the word or spelt it incorrectly, I would have to repeat the process above and try and write the word again.

I will be totally honest with you. I am not pretending it worked every time or that it was easy or that it was always fun. I spent hundreds of hours working on this when I was on public transport, and got through around half a dozen notebooks. This however, is part of having dyslexia but not letting dyslexia control me or you for that matter. If you want to learn something, you have to work 10 times harder to get the same result as everyone else. This may seem unfair, but I am telling you this is a gift. The gift of grit.

One of the biggest reasons that I didn't get the correct spelling of the word was because in my head I already knew the spelling of words I was getting wrong. I would spell words Theo's way! I always used to say,

> 'This is how it sounds, so this is how I will spell it.
> I'm not wrong, English is wrong!'

For example, if I wanted to spell the word elephant I would spell it 'elefent'. This was because that is how it sounds, and so this is how it should be spelt.

Every time I would make this mistake however, I was absorbing the incorrect spelling more and more each time, so much that it was becoming a bad habit. This needed to stop. Every time I was writing in my 'Screw Dyslexia' book I was replacing these old spellings, and breaking my old habits and putting the new habits of spelling in their place.

I was doing this alongside a sports BTEC. This was two years of a lot of computer work which of course meant... a lot of spelling mistakes.

This was just one of the things I did to help myself, but it was the one I am most proud of!

This is because it was all off my own back. I decided to do it and nobody else told me to do it or pushed me to do it. I was fully accountable for this achievement, and nobody else. There was nobody expecting me to do this, but I knew if I didn't put in the graft now and help myself, I wouldn't improve and make something of my life.

What's really stopping you?

It has to be said, that although I have put in hundreds of hours into trying to improve my English, it's still not perfect. Perfection is over-rated anyway! As I am writing this book there are loads of 'red and green lines' indicating spelling and grammar mistakes. I am aware my English will never be 100% but whose is?

I will always have to improve, which I am still doing daily little by little and I'm fine with that. The biggest problem with any diagnosis is those negative labels I have spoken about over and over again in previous chapters. We put them on ourselves because of our so called disability; the disability itself doesn't put them on us. I still have dyslexia the same as I did when I was 6 years old but nothing is stopping me writing this book, is it? Dyslexia is just slowing me down.

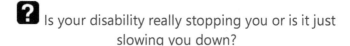 Is your disability really stopping you or is it just slowing you down?

? If it's not slowing you down, what is?

Don't become totally reliant on others.

The danger of too much help!

This is an amazing time to be alive, there has been no time in history where the word dyslexic has been so well known and accepted in society. Also, there is so much accessible technology out there that is practical and useful.

Over the last 5 years technology has dramatically advanced with inventions like voice recognition, and phones have revolutionised modern day living and have the ability to read text back to you with a click of a button. These simple inventions have changed the game for dyslexics all over the world.

These tools have been crucial for me writing this book. Without them I don't know how I could get the words onto paper, or my iPad. However, I am still finding it a challenge writing this book. I think of something in my head that makes total sense, but when I put it down on paper (or on my I-Pad), I even struggle to understand what I am saying. I have had to go over and over and over them again and again and again, speaking into Seri to get no spelling mistakes and get rid of all the red lines on the page, then I start listening to it. I do this sentence by sentence making sure each word is the word I want it to be. When I write my ideas down as they come to me there are about two to five mistakes in every sentence. Sometimes, the words aren't the right ones, the structure of it is all mucked up or it makes absolutely no sense. However, too much help can be a negative.

When listening to what I have written down and making spelling corrections by speaking into Siri on my phone sometimes she doesn't even understand me! Nor me myself! What has helped me most is having other people go over the book and correct the spelling; spot things I missed and helped structure the book so people can read and understand the main points. How I got these amazing people to help me is not by pleading with them but by passionately speaking to people about my book and them seeing the impact it could have for others with dyslexia or a similar learning difficulty. Some people offer and some people I have to ask.

When I was at Browns I became so reliant on the teacher and staff reading absolutely everything for me, except in the reading class. Sometimes I would sit there for half a lesson waiting for the teacher to read the most simple of sentences and words. I became so reliant on others that I was not exercising my reading so it did not improve. The same can happen to you with technology. This is especially true in the up and coming years as technology becomes more and more advanced and accessible.

Technology has helped me so much and sometimes too much. Having all this help with spell check, voice recognition and being able to have it speak back to you can become a trap. It's possible to become completely reliant on these great resources which will in turn dramatically decrease all your abilities and skills of memory, reading and writing. There is a fear that you can become so reliant on them we won't be able to get through life with just our ability in English alone.

But one day will come, one day you will have to read, write, and comprehend English without these tools, then what?

> What will happen then?

> *What will you do when bills come to your house?*

> *What will you do if you can't read or understand them?*

Yes, you can get by using all these great tools and never confront your dyslexia but there will come a time when it catches up with you and it can limit your possibilities and hold you back.

Don't let this happen!

Prepare yourself.

Equip yourself.

Train your brain to remember spellings and words to read at sight.

Yes of course you should go out and get all the help you can, but you must help yourself first. Throw your whole self into it, giving it your best shot, trying to learn as much as you can, until you have an understanding and more importantly confidence that you can read, even if it's just a little. If you don't have a basic understanding of English then go out and get it. Use the dyslexia book idea I have shared with you previously and take massive action and build that belief that all this technology helps you out but you are not completely reliant on it. You can cope without it.

Having said that, I am definitely not saying you should not utilise all the equipment, technology and software out there to the fullest. It is there to help you with your reading and writing, and you should definitely take advantage of whatever is available. It has changed my life. It made me so much more independent and productive. There is so much help out there these days.

Here is a list of the resources I have used to help me:

Siri (an app) on my iPhone
I have already mentioned this app many times. Every time I want or need to spell a word correctly I say it to Siri and read the spelling which appears. I then write it down somewhere either on my phone or in my book. I know everyone doesn't have an iPhone but there are equivalents out there to Siri such as Lexa for Amazon.

Getting my iPad to read back what I have written to me.
This helps me when I have written something long such as a chapter in this book. It helps me make sense of what I have written and to see if there are spelling mistakes. I do this by highlighting the paragraph and pressing the 'speak' button. You

---

Dragon software for computers or laptops.
This software is designed for people with learning disabilities such as dyslexia to increase work productivity on computers for companies. It basically does everything a keyboard does, but instead of typing, you speak into it. I used this software throughout my school life and it supported me a lot. It can be very frustrating when the 'dragon' does not understand what you are saying and sometimes I found that Siri was more accurate with understanding me. However, this could motivate you with your pronunciation of words. Another thing the Dragon Software does, is read back to you what is on the screen. I found this incredibly helpful.

In my opinion, tools such as these are all you really need. Something to help you write as well as something to help you read... what more could you want? It is like having your own personal assistant!

Chapter 22

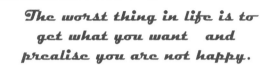

The worst thing in life is to get what you want and prealise you are not happy.

If I was to say there is one chapter in this book that would change your life more than any other, then this chapter would be it. This is why you must come back to this one chapter time and time again. It will change your life.

The stronger individual is not the one who got somewhere despite their so called disability, the stronger individual is the one who realises their gifts and strengths and above all realise they didn't get where they are despite their so called disability but ultimately they got there because of it. And because of that they see their so called disability as a gift.

If you spend your whole life fighting what you are, then you will never truly love yourself. If you don't love yourself you will never truly be happy. If you can't be happy, what else is there?

You may not be ready to fully accept this concept yet. But there will be a time when you are ready to realise that dyslexia is the biggest gift in your life and that every day that you wake up be grateful that you have this gift.

Dyslexia Is A Gift!

What I have learnt from Tony Robbins is:

In life there are 2 skills to master.

The **first** skill being the science of achievement. Becoming successful is a science, taking full responsibility of your life is a science and that's why I can give you steps and specific questions to help guide you take responsibility of your dyslexia.

The **second** skill is the art of fulfilment. Fulfilment is an art, it's not a science. What gets you fulfilled is completely different to what gets me or anyone else fulfilled. This is what most people fail to master but yet I would argue it's the most important. Realising that your so called disability is a gift in your life is part of finding fulfilment.

Most of the billionaires in the world are depressed, sad, lonely, and unfulfilled. They are unfulfilled not because they are a billionaire but because they chased the science of success thinking it will make them happy. They were wrong. But yet when I was volunteering in Nepal, living with the Nepali people in mud huts, with no heating, electricity or toilet paper all the people there were the happiest people I have ever seen because they were self-fulfilled.

What do you value more; success or fulfilment?

I can make this whole chapter about the practical gifts of dyslexia, about how it makes you see things as a whole, about how the world is heavily shaped by dyslexic people, how statistically being dyslexic means there is more of a chance for you to be wealthy and successful in your life but I'm not going to do that.

When I was attending Browns School there were posters of famous dyslexics everywhere I looked. I had teachers telling me that my dyslexia will help me out in lots of different ways and I believed that in my mind. It all made sense and was all nice and pretty. I believed that dyslexia is a gift in my head but I didn't believe it in my heart. I had to experience that dyslexia was a gift for me. So even though I thought I believed dyslexia was a gift, I never felt in my body that it was a gift. At that point in my life, (at Brown's), I didn't believe that I was lucky to have dyslexia. I always used to feel different and a bit weird that I had dyslexia.

The moment you fully realise dyslexia is a gift in your life, is when you feel it in your gut; when your eyes water every time you talk about it; when your heartbeat increases when you think about it. When it makes you smile everyday knowing that you are dyslexic. That's when you know dyslexia is a gift in your life. It's not when you just agree with someone telling you dyslexia is a gift. Until you get to that point of knowing deep down in your soul that dyslexia is a gift and that there is a reason you have it, that's when you know dyslexia is a gift. Until you reach that point, you're not there. You need to keep reading this chapter and focusing on it, focusing on improving yourself and taking actions until you really believe it.

If you take all the advice I have shared with you, answer all the questions honestly and do all the exercises then you will without doubt own and love your dyslexia and you will be an unstoppable force and achieve anything you want to achieve in your life.

However, if you believe you did all this despite your dyslexia, hate the fact you have dyslexia, and think it holds you back, then let me tell you something, you have lost my friend. You will still be hating a big, important part of your life, still not be fully happy and content in yourself. You will never be fully fulfilled.

From my experience and from all the hundreds of other dyslexic people I have met who have mastered their dyslexia, we all agree on one thing. We agree that dyslexia is a gift because it makes us who we are.

Most people don't realise the true gift of dyslexia because they still have negative labels that are covering up, blocking and hiding them from the truth that dyslexia is a gift in their life. They attach negative labels on themselves because of their dyslexia and then they can use it as an excuse. They use dyslexia as the reason to explain why they can't do something and this leads to the belief that dyslexia is limiting them in some way. They fail to see all the positive things dyslexia has led to in their life. They think they are dumb because of their dyslexia and think because of their dyslexia they won't be able to get a certain job. I used to believe that because of my dyslexia I couldn't do any job that involved a high level of reading and writing so that led me down the path to believe that the only thing I could be was a builder. I was blocking out all the ways that dyslexia was helping me.

I remember years ago when I was having a 1:1 session with a lady. She asked me –

'Theo, if you could have three wishes, have anything, what would they be?'

Without thinking I said,

> 'To have all the money in the world!'

> 'To have world peace!'

> 'To definitely not have dyslexia!'

For most of my life I wished I never had dyslexia and for most of my life I was never happy with myself; thinking there was something wrong with me, something negative about me, something not quite right with me.

 Are you judging yourself and dyslexia too soon?

 Have you been covering the true gift of dyslexia over with all your negative labels?

I am asking you this because I was guilty of this myself in the past. I was covering the true gift I had with all the labels of dumb and stupid for years and years. These were blinding me from my unique understanding of the world, from my ability to see things as a whole and being able to underpin why people do what they do. However, when I got rid of those labels and I could see my gifts for what they are, I knew I was intelligent in my own way. In some ways dyslexia and the gift of seeing this as a whole have helped me.

One area that fascinates me hugely is human behaviour and why people do what they do. I know more about human behaviour than I ever could have imagined possible. That's why I can write about the things I'm writing about. I strongly feel that I wouldn't have the same level of understanding of human behaviour if I didn't have a unique ability to look at things as a whole.

In the first 6 months of my personal training job, my understanding of the body and how everything works together exploded. When I speak to people about their posture and their alignment they are often amazed about how much I know and they see me as an expert. I don't remember most of the complex jargon when I'm coaching and training people but I have a firm understanding of the body and how to improve posture, strength and overall fitness. I feel one of the reasons I have grown so much is I have put what I learnt to the test on myself or on a willing 'guinea pig' on the gym floor. I am in no doubt that my biggest strength is being able to visualise how exactly exercise can affect the body. I think of it like I have an MRI machine in my head and that when I use it I can see how all the bones, muscles, joints and tendons work together as one unit.

About 6 months after I started my personal training job, I started volunteering in a school because I wanted to share the same messages that are in this book with others. During my first day volunteering, I keenly supported in an English lesson. I chuckled to myself as I thought it was the perfect fit! After a brief rundown of the class, I sat down next to a boy. Let's call him Tristan. This is not his real name as I can't name him for professional reasons. I noticed that his handwriting was messy and most of the words were misspelt. I also noticed he looked uncomfortable so I asked him if everything was okay.

He said:

My writing is the worst in the class!

I replied, 'I bet it's not!'

Then I pulled out a piece of paper and a pen and said to him to tell me something to write. I wrote - My name is Theo and I love English. Instantly, I turned to him and asked him whose handwriting was worse, mine or his? He said 'Yours Theo!' I went a step further and asked everyone else around the table whose was worse and they all said the same thing 'Your handwriting Theo!'

His face lit up and his smile grew bigger and bigger. With huge excitement he asked me if I had dyslexia. I said – 'Yes and I'm proud of it!' He looked a bit confused. With a big smile I said,

'We are the lucky ones!
We can do things that others can't!'

He laughed and asked me to stop joking. I replied – 'No, I'm serious! We can do things with our minds that other people can only dream of.'

Then Tristan asked me what I meant. I explained to him that dyslexics have the gift to visualise things in many different ways and from many different angles. To which he asked – 'Can't other people do that, Theo?

'No they can't,' I said 'and I can prove it to you if you want.'

He was excited and wanted to put what I had said to the test.

I asked Tristan to close his eyes and put out his hands, palms up. I asked him what his favourite cake is and he said carrot cake with a smile. Picture a slice of carrot cake in your hand Tristan, I said, and look down at it. I asked him to tell me when he had done that. Okay I'm there Tristan said. Next, I asked him to rotate the picture in his head so he was looking at the cake from underneath his hand and to tell me when he had done that. Again he said, okay I'm there. I responded – Good. Now, I want you to turn the picture you are now looking at, so that you are looking at it from the other end of the room and tell me when you have done that. Again, he said, I'm there! Now look at it from the top down, like a birds eye view. Again he was okay with that. Then came the time to open his eyes, I said to him - Only dyslexics can do that. No one else can. He was so happy and said no way and that it seemed normal for him because he had been doing it his whole life and doesn't know anything else. But he then asked how did he know nobody else could do it.

All the other children on the table were fascinated by what we were doing, so I asked them who else wanted to try it. The child next to Tristan was keen so I went through the same process with him. He was doing everything okay until I asked him to rotate the image so he was looking at the bottom of the cake. He got really confused and couldn't rotate his mental image no matter how much I helped him. I did this with three other children who were all around the table. None of them could change their mental image of the cake. Only Tristan and I could change or rotate the image of the cake in our heads.

That's when I said to him – 'See dyslexia is a gift!'

He smiled with the biggest brown eyes I have ever seen and said –

'I love having dyslexia!'

This is one of the special gifts of dyslexia and I have used it to help me in my life.

You can take full responsibility of your dyslexia by peeling off all your old labels and use dyslexia to your advantage. If you do all of this but then still do not like the fact that you are dyslexic you have given up all hope of loving yourself and ever thinking you are someone special.

As you know from earlier chapters, I wasn't always this way. Even after I passed my English GCSE and felt on top of the world, I didn't feel the same way then as I do now about my dyslexia. I still thought it was something that was holding me back, something I had to fight all my life.

I now know that thinking differently is such a gift.

Albert Einstein and Leonardo Da Vinci were dyslexic.

Do you think Albert and Leonardo would have helped change the world if they didn't have dyslexia?

I really doubt it.

Their intelligence was a gift because they were different. Think about it! There is lots more opportunities for you because you think differently. If you think the same way as everyone else then you will live a normal life just like everyone else, but you have the gift of never experiencing an average life.

Celebrate your differences because there is more opportunity for you out there.
Who wants to be normal anyway?
It's boring! Way over rated!

The moment my life changed forever was a couple of months after I passed my GCSE English. One morning, in early October, I was walking my dogs, doing my hour of power and started wondering why my life was the way that it was. I was wondering why I was so excited about my life. Why couldn't I wait to get home from school every day and work on my ideas, my dreams, my goals and why my friends just wanted to go out and have fun and party all the time? The answer I came up with is because I was and still am motivated about my personal development, growing and maximising my life.

Okay fair enough I thought but then I asked myself - what got me into personal development in the first place? After some thought I realised that it was because I watched and got influenced by Tony Robins whose words,

'The only way to change your life is to take responsibility of your life.'

really hit home and struck a chord.

I know I have shared this with you in previous chapters but when I found myself in a deep negative hole it was such a low point in my life and I had to find a way out and to make my life better. In that whole I had trouble speaking to people, I felt crippling shyness; I was being bullied at school. I felt so lost and alone at school and I absolutely hated my life. I felt that I was so different to everyone else.

After a while, I got fed up of being lost and alone so I asked myself the question - how can I change it? That's when I found Tony Robbins who gave me the tools for me to take responsibility of my life and my so called disability. I got out of the deep hole and found myself in a higher place than ever before. I asked myself WHY? The answer I came up with changed my life forever. I realised that I felt so different, so shy, so lost because I had the special gift of dyslexia and I was the lucky one! In that very moment I started crying. That very moment everything changed. I realised that my dyslexia is the reason I took responsibility of my life. Dyslexia is the reason I'm on the path I'm on. It's the reason I'm so excited about my life. Without dyslexia I wouldn't have developed the discipline and the hunger to get up at 3am regularly and transform my life. Without dyslexia I wouldn't be the proud man I am today. From that moment on I knew that dyslexia was nothing less than my greatest gift.

I transformed my life by asking myself the question of why my life was the way it was.

Make your life something to be proud of.

Discover that dyslexia makes you the person you are today.

The key questions I asked myself were and you need to ask yourself are:

Why is my life so different/better than everyone else's?
Your answer:

_____

Why is that then?

Your answer:

_____

And again - Why is that then?
Your answer:

_____

Here is mine as an example:

Why is my life so different to everyone else's?
My answer: because I have so many goals in my life. I'm
excited to go home and work on myself and my goals.

Why is that then?
My answer: because I have got obsessed with personal
development and taking responsibility for my life.

And again - Why is that then?
My answer: because I felt so lost at school and felt down
and hated my life that I had to do something and look for
something to improve it.

And, again, why is that then?
My answer: because I don't think the same as everyone
else, and I find certain things hard, I'm dyslexic.

Ask why again and again and again, keep digging until
you discover the fundamental reason. Don't worry or
overthink it. You will just know when you are there. Your
emotions will take over and you will have such strong
conviction that you just know it's true.

I know some of you might not be ready for this step and
are still thinking 'How can this be a gift?' I know exactly
how you feel. I have been there and as you know I spent
many years thinking dyslexia is a curse. I was wishing
every day that I would wake up and not have dyslexia. It

made me feel like I had an illness; a ball and chain around my neck.

You might not be ready to accept this yet. You may not be ready to accept that your dyslexia is actually your greatest gift. **Remember**, it's your responsibility to create what things mean to you. **Remember**, you decide what the meaning is of things. Now, I want you to challenge yourself to uncover, discover and create the true meaning of dyslexia in your life. Answer this question.

Dyslexia is a 'what' in my life?

After answering this then come up with all your reasons for why dyslexia is that in your life. Remember, the more reasons the stronger it is.

Dyslexia is _____in my life because

_____

Another example of mine:
Dyslexia is a gift in my life because it makes me who I am. It makes me think differently. It helps me visualise things better

How can anyone realise that dyslexia is a gift?

The fact remains that there are some of you who are reading or listening to this who are not fully ready to have a breakthrough with your dyslexia and realise it's a gift in your life. If you have got rid of all your old labels and no longer believe it's stopping you, then it comes down to just a matter of focus.

Next you need to decide what controls your focus more than anything else.

Questions control our focus more than anything else, so if

you want to improve your focus in a particular area then just ask habitual questions related to that area. For example, if you want to become a better runner you would probably ask yourself - 'How can I become a better runner?' on a consistent basis.

Remember, that the mind works like a muscle and the more you do or feel something the easier it is to do that thing or feel that emotion. We can use this understanding and incorporate it into our questions so you can begin to realise how much dyslexia is a gift in your life.

If you just answer these questions once, then you will feel good about your dyslexia once or for a short period of time. But if we ask these questions on a habitual base, like every morning then you will focus more.

Every morning, you could ask yourself something like:
- What is something I can do that others find hard or can't do?
- What can I appreciate about dyslexia?
- What have I learnt because I have dyslexia?
- I am grateful that I have dyslexia because ___?

By asking these questions day after day and writing down the answers you can see them in front of you. You will start to believe, really think and feel dyslexia is a gift.

Answer these questions every morning:

What can I appreciate about dyslexia?

What can I do that others find hard or can't do?

What have I learnt because I have dyslexia?

I am grateful that I have dyslexia because..........

Dyslexia is a gift in my life because…….

Yet another **example of mine**:

What can I appreciate about my dyslexia? I appreciate
how it makes me think in a holistic way, that most people
can't.

What can I do that others find hard or can't do? I find
it easy to understand why people are doing what they are
doing because I find it easy to see things from others
point of view. Others can't do this anywhere near as well
and they get angry at others because they can't see things
from their point of view.

What have I learnt because I have dyslexia? I learnt
things about the body and the mind in a more overall
way.

I am grateful that I have dyslexia because… I am
grateful for the fact it has introduced me to lots of people
who are willing to help me read and write.

Dyslexia is a gift in my life because it has shaped my
character, gave me the gift of grit to push past what feels
hard and made me really good at dealing with problems.

Remember!
Even if you don't truly believe in your heart that dyslexia
is a gift, just begin to ask yourself questions, write down
the answers with a state of certainty and expectancy.

Remember, whatever questions you ask you will find an
answer to. Answer the questions above every morning
before you do anything else because in the morning your
mind is the most suggestible and a morning ritual is the
most powerful habit you can develop.

I promise you if you do this every day and write down all the answers, after a month or so you will feel transformed and you will love the fact that you have dyslexia.

Chapter 23

Step 11 - Realise the gift of dyslexia.

What do you want to do?
Who do you want to be for your life?

I see so many young and even older people not knowing what they want to do in their life. I used to find it crazy and stupid that they still don't know what they want in life but now I understand. I understand why they don't. It's because they don't truly look, they don't look at all the real possibilities that are out there. They limit their potential and say I can't do that, or that's unlikely or not realistic. It's the limiting labels of themselves that are holding them back and stopping them fully committing to doing what they want to do in life. But that's not you, you have broken past your limiting labels and if you still see them creeping back into your life and you will. You can shove them aside and say,

'I know and I believe that my potential is limitless!'

Now that just leaves you with where to start. One piece of advice! Don't try to be perfect or choose the right thing, just start now. Do the next thing that you see that will make you grow and open you up to new experiences because once you see yourself in a new experience you find out more about yourself - who you are, what you like, your strengths and weaknesses. And through these seamlessly random experiences you will find your passion. You will find something you want to do well in.

Go at that one thing with everything you've got. Try your best to master that one thing, even if you think it's not what you will be doing forever because the fact is you most likely will change direction or it might not work out. You might even fail but that's okay. Just go full on at everything you have a passion for and trust me you will love where you end up and what path it takes you down.

Where I Am Now

I want to finish by saying where I am now; where my journey with dyslexia has taken me. As you know the outcome of this book is for you to take responsibility of your so called disability and for you to realise that your so called disability is your greatest gift. Before I finish I want to share with you why I've taking this path with helping people with dyslexia instead of becoming a full time personal trainer or any other profession. I simply hope and believe it will help you and others develop your own path in life.

At the age of 14, when I found out about the job of a personal trainer that was all I wanted to be. When I fully took responsibility of my life and got obsessed with personal development, I wanted to know more about the nutrition and the food we eat and what effect it is having on our bodies. But I had a problem! I couldn't get it from a book! However, I didn't let that stop me! I looked into audio books. The first audio book I listened to was called 'The China Study.'

It's an internationally famous health book, predicated about having a plant based diet. One of the messages in this book is that the growth of cancer can be stopped if you stop eating animal protein and live on a plant based diet. Naively, without much thinking I believed the book whole heartedly and took it for what it said. I wanted to help the world and this gave me a way to do that. I came up with the goal of starting my own charity and clinic to help people who had been diagnosed with cancer. I wanted to help them recover and be healthier by not eating any animal products. I was so excited and I went at it with full force.

As I shared the study with others many questions were asked. This made me think further and really think about the message of no animal products equals no cancer. One day I started doing more research into the book and found out that it's not a pure cure and it doesn't work all the time. It felt like my whole life plans were gone. In high and sight I should have done a lot more reading and study before taking it for what was in black and white in the book. I learnt an invaluable lesson with this experience.

After a couple of months of my life being turned upside down when I was 17, I had enough and refocused and reenergised myself. I saw my idle Tony Robbins for the first time in a two day seminar. On the last day of the seminar I got inspired and signed up to an email marketing course so I could start earning some extra income; which by the way, never happened!

At the same time I was looking into becoming a health coach/ life coach. I dived deep into phycology and started to understand more about how the brain works. My reason or goal was to help make people all over the world healthier. I did this alongside studying for my personal training course and getting my C in English.

One day in January 2017, 6 months after I got my C in English I was going to a free one to one life coaching session in London Bridge. The gentleman leading the session was in a black suit and I was in my nicest tracksuit. Ted Middleman was his name.

'So Theo tell me a little about yourself', he said for the opening question.

'Errrr!' I didn't know what to say. After a few

minutes, 'Well I'm one of the worst dyslexics in England…' and began speaking all about how I improved my dyslexia with no help compared to having the best help in the world. If anything I had planned to speak about my personal training and life coaching.

After my passionate rant Ted replied by saying,

> *Theo, you have a unique ability to help others with dyslexia, you should write a book about what you have learnt and about your experience with dyslexia so others can do the same.*

After the meeting I was killing some time walking along the river Thames in deep thought about how I would move forward with my life, which path to take.

I had some ideas about how I could incorporate both helping people with their health/ fitness and helping people with their dyslexia. But no matter how I thought about it, it wasn't gaining any traction. Then I got out my notebook from my bag and I wrote down a question at the top of a page -

What
do
I want
to do
with my life?

I instinctively wrote down '**help people**'. When I feel like I'm helping people, that's when I am most happy and fulfilled. I believe that this is what gets the best out of everybody. When you are giving you have more to give compared to when you are just doing it for yourself.

Tony Robbins says life will support whatever supports more of life. This just means that if you do things for others, you will be supported. When you see happy and successful people at work, it's because they are doing something that has a higher meaning than them. They are helping others and because they are focused on that, they have more to give.

This is why my answer was to help people and I suggest you write down your answer to this question. And then I asked myself,

'What can I do that will help the most people?'

Next thing I did when sitting on the bench figuring out my life plan was, write down all the things I wanted to do with my life.

My list looked like this:

- *my dyslexia mission,*
- *personal training,*
- *marketing myself through email,*
- *coaching,*
- *health coaching,*
- *public speaking.*

Next, I asked myself,

Where can I help the most people and where is there the most need?

What's my true gift?

What can I do that no one else can do or has done?

The answer was so obvious; my dyslexia mission.

I needed to make it my mission to share my breakthrough and teach as many people as I can. Teach and share the two fundamental principles that changed my life so that others can do the same and take back their life.

I decided not to become the best personal trainer I could be and not make that my full-time career. I knew that there were enough personal trainers out there and there was nothing that is extra special that I could offer if I fully focused on fitness and the body. It seemed so obvious when I realised I had something special to add. There is no one who I have come across or read about giving the same message that I am giving.

This is the path I took myself down – it's your turn.
Next, answer these questions.

> **Q.** What do you want to do or what is your biggest dream for yourself to become?
>
> **Q.** What are all the ways you can get there?
>
> **Q.** What will make you unique?
>
> **Q.** What will help the most people in a meaning full way?

Chapter 24

The gift of thinking differently!

Dyslexia is not just a big gift for us, it is a big gift for mankind.

This chapter is about the gift of thinking differently. It explains why, thinking and behaving differently means there is a greater opportunity out there for you.

The world would not be the same if there was no such thing as dyslexia.

Having dyslexia means your brain works differently to everyone else's. This means we notice different things in the same situation. I used to describe dyslexia as it's like going to see a movie with somebody but you are seeing a completely different film. I would walk out of that movie with a completely different understanding or experience, I would notice different things, find different things funny or not, mostly different to than my friend who wasn't dyslexic.

The simple fact that we think differently means that there is more of an opportunity for us. It makes us more unique. It makes us rarer; more valuable once you are using the skills of dyslexia to their best.

Remember this does not just apply for dyslexics but it also applies for those with autism, ADHD, or any other so-called learning disability or any so-called disability for that matter.

The most famous dyslexic is arguably Albert Einstein who was a ground-breaking theoretical physicist and Nobel Prize winner.

He is known as the father of modern quantum physics. When I was growing up at Browns, his name was everywhere.

Everywhere you looked sayings like –

If
Albert Einstein can overcome his dyslexia and become the genius he is, you can do the same.

This was invaluable when I was growing up. He was and still is a role model and he gave me confidence. But I would say that they got one thing wrong!

Albert Einstein didn't become successful despite his dyslexia; he became successful because of it.

He didn't overcome his dyslexia and find ways around it. He learnt to use his dyslexia to his advantage and learnt to apply it to his work. His dyslexia gave him the gift to see things in such a unique way that no one else on the face of this earth had seen.

As a child Einstein suffered from a number of learning disabilities including severe memory issues, dyslexia and being a late talker. At school he was a rebel, a loner and he didn't go to most of his classes. In fact, he was so slow when learning to talk that his parents consulted doctors and some of his teachers used to say to him he would never amount to anything.

As he grew up Einstein became deeply curious, passionate and persistent in understanding the underlying laws of the universe. He had a very strong visual mind and learning process, and had an extraordinary ability to take extremely complex problems and break them down into simple ideas which were often the basis for his thought experiments.

Does he remind you of anybody?

His ability to break down complex problems is a common

gift most dyslexics experience. His ability to engage in school is similar for most dyslexics too. Einstein chose not to go to classes, not to make any friends and he learnt best visually with pictures instead of words.

Do you think he could have been persistent without developing the gift of grit?

Do you think Einstein would still have got obsessed with understanding the universe if he learnt at the same level as everybody else? I don't think so.

1. His speech was delayed.

Like many people with dyslexia, Einstein was a late talker. He didn't start speaking comfortably until he was nearly 6 years old.

2. He struggled with reading, writing, maths and languages.

He struggled with reading aloud and with finding the right words to use. He also found it hard to express his thoughts and ideas on paper. His poor ability with maths and his lack of ability in any academic subject led some of his teachers to predict that 'nothing good' would come of him. Despite this, Einstein worked extremely hard and persevered in doing his maths homework, even though he often came up with the wrong answers. Through this he developed the gift of grit.

3. He learned better in creative environments.

Many people with dyslexia learn best when they're able to learn in a creative way. Einstein had a hard time at school. His learning relied a lot on memory and rote learning. Just like me, he did very well after switching to a new school that encouraged creative thinking and learning.

4. He saw the world from a unique perspective.

People with learning differences naturally think outside

the box. Albert Einstein was no exception. His ability to think creatively meant he came up with ideas that other scientists hadn't imagined, like $E = MC^2$!

At the age of 16, Einstein was sitting in a maths class; bored and daydreaming. He looked at the clock and then he asked himself a simple question –

How do we know what time it is?

Then he thought, well we look at the clock.

Next, he thought about how he could see the clock. In his head he remembered previous science lessons and worked out the process - the light bounces off the clock and into my eyes. Einstein then asked himself a third question, that only a dyslexic person would ask

What would happen if you could travel at the speed of light?

If it travelled with the light, sitting on the end of that beam of light, then what would I see? He imagined and visualised being on the end of the beam of light. He guessed that what he would actually see would be the time change on the clock and the hand move from one second to another. His curiosity unsatisfied, he asked himself a fourth question. Another question a non-dyslexic would never ask.

He asked himself…

What if we travelled faster than the beam of light? What would we see then?
What if we travelled faster than all the other light ways?

His thoughts were:

Well I wouldn't see the clock moving from one to two, I guess I would see the clock moving back from 1pm to 12noon. Then he asked the final and fundamental question that would change not only his life but consequently the life of millions of others. He asked, would I see the clock moving back from 1pm to 12noon or would I actually be seeing time moving backwards because I'm going faster than light itself and would I be moving back in time? Einstein got obsessed with this question for years and years until he scientifically backed it up with numbers, equations and tests.

Do you think you could have thought of those answers to those questions?

Of course you could have. The only difference is Einstein thought of the question first because he thought differently to everyone else of his time. People who are different change the world. So called normal people just live in the world that we different people create.

Einstein and his brilliant dyslexic mind didn't stop there. He came up with 'Thought Experiments' that changed the scientific world and therefore changed the physical world. These experiments expanded very complex ideas and concepts in a simple way so everyone could understand them.

He thought of an experiment to explain how light works and the famous equation of how $E = MC^2$ which explains the Theory of Relativity.

We use his findings for almost everything. Without him our GPS Navigation System would be off by a couple of minutes. Because they used the Theory of Relatively to calculate the times, it is now very accurate. This is just one example of a great man using his great dyslexic mind.

Chapter 25

The world is shaped by people who think differently to the norm, bask in that glory and enjoy being different and find your thing.

This chapter looks at what famous and successful dyslexics said about their dyslexia and how it helped and continues to help them.

We will look at:

Richard Branson,
Steven Spielberg,
Whopping Goldberg,
Orlando Bloom,
Henry Winkler,
Jay Leno,
Jame Oliver,
Daymond John,
Eddie Izzard and
Kevin O' Leary.

These are living proof
that
the world is shaped by people
who think differently
to the norm.

Richard Branson

When I was at school I would look at a blackboard and not understand anything on that blackboard and at age 15 I decided to leave school. I just couldn't do any exams. I was hopeless.

When I went out into the real world and I came across things that I was interested in. I think I could get a better grasp on it than most people and because I was a dyslexic I was also very good at finding other really good people. Surrounding myself with good people who could compensate for my weaknesses and it taught me to be a very good delegator, which is very important if you are running businesses. I think, the advice I give to mothers who have got dyslexic children is let them, don't force them too hard on the things they find difficult. They will exceed, excel on some other areas. Push them into those other areas. A lot of the most successful people in the world were once or are dyslexic.

From my 20s, I started talking about the fact that I'd discovered that I was dyslexic. I did it on purpose because I think it's important for others, especially young kids who have been told they are dyslexic to see that there is successful people who get through it and if they follow their particular dreams, follow what they are good at, they can be even more successful at what they are good at than others. And there are so many people like myself who have excelled in their individual professions who are dyslexic. So I think it's really important that people who are dyslexic get out and talk about it.

I'm dyslexic and therefore I think I have been very good at keeping things simple because as a dyslexic I need things to be simple for myself. Therefore Virgin I think, when we launch a financial service company or bank we do not use jargon and everything is very clear cut and very simple. I think people have an infinity to the Virgin brand because we don't talk above them or talk down to them.

Steven Spielberg

As having been dyslexic for my entire life, which explained a lot of things. It was like the last puzzle part, ended tremendous mystery that I've kept to myself all these years. It basically started with just things that happened when you are a kid in school, and you're a slow reader and in my case I was actually unable to read for,

for at least 2 years. I was 2 years behind the rest of my class and of course I went through what everybody goes through; the teasing and I had to go through that for a long time and so the teasing you know, led to a lot of other problems I was having in school but it all stemmed from the fact that I was embarrassed to stand-up in front of the class and… and read. But I never felt like a victim, that was the important thing, I never felt like a victim. I think movies really helped me, they kind of saved me from shame, from guilt, from putting it on myself and it was really, you know, you know my own burden. It wasn't my burden, and I think making movies was my great escape, that's really how I was able to get away from all of that.

Interviewer: And do you think that you show through your movies, you show how you felt or just what you felt about the world or what you felt about people teasing you, I guess for what you were going through?

Steve: Not really! My first movies didn't do that. My first movie was just basically imitations of movies that I was going out to theatres to see. They were pure you know, genre movies, war movies, Westerns, science-fiction and, there were no statements. I made no statements; I'm talking about my 9 millimetre movies. I'm going way back to before I became a director. And I'm just saying that in light of feeling a little bit like an outsider, movies made me feel inside my own skill set. And the other thing is I'm in a business right now where reading is very important, you know it's of critical importance to me that I read books and scripts and, so I've been able to over compensate. I just basically with no… with never feeling ashamed of myself will take 2 hours and 45 minutes to 3 hours to read 120 pages. It takes me about 2 hours 45 minutes to read what most people read in about an hour and 10 minutes. I just know I'm still slow at reading but I have learnt to adjust. I read often but I'm very…. here is a great thing also; I have great comprehension of what I read because I do read slowly. I retain almost everything I read. I don't just skip over things and I'm able to appreciate the writing and I'm able to really savour good writing because I really take my time going through a book or a script.

Interviewer: If you had any advice to give for young kids who have dyslexia and who are just finding out what they are going through now, what would you tell them?

Steven – Just that it's more common than you ever could imagine and that you are not alone and that there are ways to accelerate your reading skills, to accelerate your comprehension and there are ways to deal with this. It's not a curable thing. It's something you are going to have the rest of your life but you can, sort of, dart between the rain drops to get where you what to go and it will not hold you back.

Whoopi Goldberg

Interviewer: Do you think your dyslexia has got you to where you are today?

Whoopi - I'm sure it had a large hand in it, and the fact that since I was born I have always known. I want to pretend to put myself in other time periods to be able to pretend to be another species. That stuff to me is interesting and it helps my mind expand.

Interviewer: It's our way of escaping the real life, and I think normal people can't really do that, they have a harder time.

Whoopi – I think they have a very hard time with that, I feel bad for them.

I think the advantage is my brain sees and puts information in my head differently. Ah, sometimes more interestingly I think than if I saw like everyone else. I think it's less challenging now because we have some idea about it but I think the challenge will always be how we see ourselves. Not as folks for the handicap, but folks with an interesting perspective on everything.

Orlando Bloom

Just hold on to your dreams and never ever think you are not good enough or that you are stupid. You know never let anyone tell you that you are stupid or that you know that you are not capable because it's a human issue isn't it? It's like it is mostly a human issue. We are all the same; we are all equal, you know and we deserve a shot, and I would just say, take this obstacle and make it the reason to have a big life. Because if you can climb and if you overcome that obstacle you are going to be that much further ahead than anyone else because it takes having obstacles to learn and grow and be better. It's like, if it was smooth, plain sailing what have you become, if you are a straight A-student maybe that's great. But I'm sure there are many straight A-students who end up smoking pot, taking…. You know what I mean? But the obstacle, the mountain that is the challenge of climbing that dyslexia, is something that you can make it your own and make it your reason that you are a winner in life.

Henry Winkler

Interviewer(BBC news): You found out you had dyslexia, but way later on in your life.

Henry: Right, I found out when I was 31. You know what inspired me, here is the thing. I felt horrible growing up. I always felt on the outside. I always felt like I was stupid, like I couldn't figure out concepts. And what my message is, is you have greatness in you. Not one of the children sitting here does not have greatness in them, and it is really important that they know that and that school is the law. Maybe school is difficult but when you get out, you sore like an eagle.

It is not the money, it's just the way you see the child as an individual and what it is they need, and it's not a matter of cuddling, it's not a matter of spoiling but a heard child to me is a powerful child. If a child feels like somebody is paying attention they feel differently about themselves. That's just the truth.

So let me just say to all the children that are listening. Every one of you is powerful, and school does not define you. You define yourself. I'm not kidding. You're wonderful.

<u>Jay Leno</u>

(Setting: Jay's school from years ago)

Interviewer: What was it like being in here and not being the smartest kid in the class?

Jay: You know we didn't call it dyslexia then, it was called smarten up, smarten up, and smarten up.

Jay's brother: Jay is dyslexic and you know he spent a lot of his time in the principal's office for playing pranks or laying rubber in the parking lot. I think his parents were very concerned about what was going to happen to him.

Jay: You know, I had a wonderful teacher, English teacher, named Mrs Hark. She said 'I always see you telling stories and making jokes. Why don't you take my creative writing class and I'll give you a credit in English for that and you write some of these stories down and maybe you could read them to the class.

Interviewer: Did that change you at all?

Jay: Yer it did because it was the first time in my life that I actually focused on something. When I would do homework, it would be, okay 16x5. What's that? A fly. I wonder where it's going? I mean I would never focus on anything. So that was the first time in my life I think I really focused on something.

Brother: He turned out to be the famous one, the rich one, and I think he did that because he worked so hard.

Jamie Oliver

Interviewer: Did they try and encourage you to be better or did they sweep you to the side?

Jamie: No I went to special needs classes which had about 4 kids that went, had special extra classes and stuff. Yer my teachers were lovely but I don't think that we were as strategically as advanced as we are now. I think we are much better at it now. But also we didn't recognise dyslexia. It was like an on-off button. You were either dyslexic and you had to literally be looking through 2 inch glasses or you're not. I think now we know there are many forms of it and I don't think I'm deeply held back by dyslexia. Undoubtedly, I've got it but you know, I think I was giving all the support for the time. It just wasn't my place to shine really.

I had a kid come up to me the other day… and… you sometimes read about stuff like this but you don't think it's a real emotion. This kid must have been about 10 and he came up to me and said I heard you are dyslexic. I said yes I am. He asked have you ever felt that you were worth nothing? And I'm like…. No, why? Why do you think that? Do you feel that? And he's like… yer. That's the stage where you got to start worrying because it doesn't; you know being dyslexic or having any special need is not an excuse or a reason for you to not prosper. It's just you're not going to be good at the predictable things. But you know, I mean there are wonderful people who do business and architecture and art and music that have had learning difficulties. But I think what that kid was tapping into is that every single one of us need to feel like we are good at something otherwise we fell like shit. You know he obviously did. So I had a little pep talk with him for sort of 10 minutes and hopefully, hopefully it made a difference. I told him to come and see me when he was 16. I said I'd give him a job. Really what I was talking about was self-esteem. That can be relevant to anyone, regardless of dyslexia or not really... but...

<u>Daymond John</u>

After I started to talk about just being dyslexic and as I researched it I have to really look at it and say it's an asset. Am and I think the asset is that when I had to read something, I had to read it 5 times. When I saw the opportunity of co-op; to go to school one week and to work the other I went to work. I always just visualised and concentrated on things because maybe the theory is we're not getting... dyslexics don't get caught up reading books and reading how it should be done and go out and execute how it should be done. It's funny, I walk into a room, I'll do a speaking gig in front of 5,000 people and I'd say - How many people in here are dyslexic? Four people raise their hand. Right. It's usually the CEOs and very, very powerful people that raise their hand but people that work within environments, they are ashamed and they are afraid and they don't share. Then I start to give them stats about Will Smith, Tom Cruise, and myself and the 4 sharks all of a sudden everyone in the room is dyslexic and raising their hand. But I just want obviously to bring this awareness to people.

Interviewer: And it's nothing to be ashamed of.

Raymond: Absolutely not and you know I would want to make sure people get tested that if they feel that there's a challenge, a learning challenge.

Eddie Izzard

Okay so dyslexia you might have this, and teachers you might see kids who might be suffering with this. You can look this stuff up, you can get help and stuff gets better in life so if you are having a tough time of it now, don't worry about it too much but reach out and talk to parents, talk to friends, talk to teachers, talk to everyone and as a hashtag, you can look this up, #youknowadyslexic. You know a dyslexic, they have to spell that. They have to spell know. It's tricky, it should just be ping, it should just be hashtag ping but its #youknowdyslexia. Anyway there's the hashtag, put that in and you win a sausage, and you can get your life back and stuff will come up, yes. Yes stuff will come up on that which will help you.

Things can get better and will get better but you have to take action upon it. ACTION. Do things to make this change and then you can be a crazy person like me and have painted finger nails and living and talking with the words that were the problem with the spelling and you have been giving things that looks like a negative, but you can turn it into a positive. That's my message to you. Take this, stick it in your pipe and smoke it.

Thank you. Goodbye.

Kevin O' Leary

Interviewer: You're dyslexic?

Kevin – Yes.

Interviewer: You learned that at a pretty young age?

Kevin: I am dyslexic and very, very much so. It was very

challenging for me. I couldn't read in the early ages and it really affects your reading score and gets you pushed back. But there was a woman named Marjory Golic who is very famous, out of university Migil with Sambenevich. I became a part of an experimental class. They were testing an idea at the time and it was my mother that got me in that class. She kind of made sure I got in there somehow and I thank her so much for it. There thesis went like this. You feel so weird when you are dyslexic because, and I can still do this, I can read upside down, I can read in a mirror, and what Marjory said was; look this is not a fault, you have a superpower. And when you're that young you buy into that and it gives you the confidence you need and that's what's occurred to me.

Interviewer: And that carried you a long way?

Kevin: Yer...

Interviewer: It makes you so emotional. Why is that?

Kevin: Excuse me. It's just when I think of those days..

Interviewer: I think when people only see your hard shell and they probably think that you never ran into challenges like that.

Kevin: They were tough times; very tough times because I was really wondering if I was going to ever make it. It was you know, those were very tough times. I was failing. There was a lot of panic in my own family, my teachers weren't sure. And I knew it was err very lucky, I was very lucky. I meet lots of dyslexic people today and I give them encouragement because **it is a superpower.**

DEDICATION
To mum and dad for fighting the battle that I never could have; you did a great job!